BEFORE BURNOUT

BEFORE
BURNOUT
BALANCED LIVING FOR BUSY PEOPLE

by

Frank Minirth, M.D.
Don Hawkins, Th.M.
Paul Meier, M.D.
Chris Thurman, Ph.D.

MOODY PRESS
CHICAGO

Library of Congress Cataloging in Publication Data

Before burnout / by Don Hawkins . . . [et al.].
    p.   cm.
  ISBN 0-8024-0879-6
  1. Burn out (Psychology)—Religious aspects—Christianity.
2. Christian life—1960-   3. Obsessive-compulsive disorder.
I. Hawkins, Don. II. Title: Before burn out.
BV4509.5.B44   1990
158'.1-dc20   89-28715
                                           CIP

5 7 9 10 8 6

Printed in the United States of America

To our many good friends
from among the obsessive-compulsives
whose lives have impacted and
shaped us to balance our obsessions
by living life one day at a time
with an eye on eternity

CONTENTS

FOREWORD

When most of us take the time to read a book on burnout, we look for it to do at least two things: present concepts clearly enough so anyone can understand them and compel us to change and/or renewal.

I found that both these elements abound in *Before Burnout*. This is the second in a great series by these authors, and each book has helped me rediscover two life-changing truths that are essential to beating burnout.

I speak from the heart here. I never realized how easy it is to slip into burnout, but I've also suffered from what the authors say is its number one cause: unfulfilled expectations. That *fact* wasn't new to me, but the *skills* needed to detect the subtle ways it can creep into your life were; and that's what makes both these books so valuable.

In *How to Beat Burnout*, I was taken on a journey that helped me rediscover the thousands of expectations I had. It offered valuable insights on how to cope with the tremendous emotional burden unfulfilled expectations can create in life. Those were sobering lessons for me, especially because I travel the country teaching people the damage unfulfilled expectations can bring to their lives and relationships. Somehow, I failed to see the overwhelming number of expectations I had allowed to be a part of my life.

To my amazement, I realized I had expectations about everything: traffic flow, store clerks, machines, government employees, my family, my staff, how many people should attend our seminars, read our books, rent our film series—the list could go on. No wonder I was burned out!

But the good doctors didn't just leave me hanging by a thread. After insightfully helping me realize where I was, they skillfully guided me back to where I needed to be—firmly resting on the marvelous truth of Isaiah 40:31. "Yet those who wait for the Lord will gain new strength; they will mount up with wings like eagles, they will run and not get tired, they will walk and not become weary."

Before Burnout nobly takes the torch from its predecessor and offers gems that can help you beat burnout *before* it happens. Each intriguing chapter will take you through the pages of Scripture and shine a clear, transparent light on the secrets to heading burnout off at the pass.

In reading this book I was reminded of two of my favorite truths about contentment. The first is, *if we're not satisfied with what we have today, we'll never be satisfied with what we want tomorrow.* The second is equally powerful, *contentment is knowing I already have everything I need in Christ.*

In this worthy sequel, Drs. Meier, Minirth, and Thurman, along with their good friend and long-time colleague Don Hawkins, give us the knowledge we need to believe these truths and the skills necessary to apply them.

There are more books out there on burnout than any of us have time to read; but this one is worth your time. Learning how to beat burnout before it beats us is something we all need help with; you're holding a tool right now that can help you do that. If you're grappling with the same issues of peace, contentment, and fulfillment I have, this book is for you.

GARY SMALLEY

PREFACE

The purpose of our previous book, *How to Beat Burnout*, was to address a problem that has reached epidemic proportions in today's society: burnout. In that book we showed burnout victims how to overcome their burned-out condition and return to successful Christian living.

In this book we zero in on one of the three major causes of burnout—an obsessive-compulsive personality, along with related Type A characteristics—to show individuals with those traits how they can prevent their tendencies from resulting in an initial or cyclical burnout.

We know a group of obsessive-compulsive individuals who regularly check themselves by asking, "Why be 'O-C' about this situation?" In other words, they ask, "Is it really necessary for me to practice extreme obsessive-compulsive—hard-driving and perfectionistic—behavior in this situation?"

The answer clearly is no. It isn't necessary to be O-C in our work, thought, and actions to prove to God or to other people the worth of our work or ourselves, which is the general motivation for O-C behavior. The alternative is to be the person God wants us to be today.

To do that, we will take a close look at how the obsessive-compulsive and Type A personalities think, feel, and act, and how their tendencies toward extremes in certain areas can become more balanced. In today's society we see more and more individuals with obsessive-compulsive personality traits, so it's likely that you are among them or interact closely with someone who is. We cannot give individuals with these personality traits entirely new personalities, nor would we want to. But we do hope to show how they can adjust their more extreme and potentially harmful traits so that they can experience more balanced and fulfilling lives.

Part of this book was written during a hurried plane trip. The last part was written sometime later during a restful Saturday afternoon at a Bible conference. In between were a number of personal struggles with obsessive-compulsive behavior, of which we all will undoubtedly experience more. But the process of writing this book has helped enlighten us and give us direction in overcoming our own obsessive behavior. We trust that this beginning in our own lives will extend to those who read this book.

After all, why be so O-C when it is healthier and biblical to be more balanced in our behavior? May we all gain the insight and motivation to make balanced living a daily reality.

1
THE BURNOUT-PRONE
PERSONALITY

Several staff members of a Christian radio station had been working almost nonstop for weeks to develop a multi-media presentation for a Christian college. Hundreds of slides had been taken, processed, selected, and carefully sorted. They had recorded interviews with numerous individuals. Thousands of feet of audio tape had been auditioned and edited. The staff had worked hard to select carefully a wide variety of background music. Finally, all the ingredients were coming together.

As they neared the end of the project, the exhausted crew stopped about three o'clock one afternoon for a quick bite of lunch. Turning to his secretary, the project manager said, "Debi, why don't you ask God's blessing on this food."

"Sure" she replied, then quickly prayed, "God, help us to get everything done, now please, and in order. Amen." Immediately the crew broke into laughter.

"What's so funny?" asked the manager.

His administrative assistant replied, "Why, that was the perfect workaholic's prayer. That is *exactly* what you would expect from a group of obsessive-compulsives* like us."

Sometimes being obsessive-compulsive is stimulating, interesting, and a lot of fun. Many times it can be highly productive. Our research at the Minirth-Meier Clinic has shown us that obsessive-compulsive individuals tend to be the most productive, conscientious workers.

But obsessive-compulsive (perfectionistic) behavior can be destructive, both to obsessive-compulsives and to those around them. Though obsessive-compulsives are unlikely to fail at a job through irresponsibility, carelessness, or neglect, they are likely to bring about a catastrophe by working themselves to the point of burnout. In fact, this book came into existence partially as a result of the harried experience of those radio-station workaholics putting together that multimedia presentation.

THE CHRISTIAN TENDENCY TOWARD BURNOUT

Although obsessive-compulsive personality traits can be seen in men and women, college students and farmers, hard driving executives and overstressed housewives, a large percentage of evangelical Christians have an overabundance of obsessive-compulsive personality traits.

One such workaholic was Paul Meier. We'll let him tell his own story.

> When I first started my residency in psychiatry at Duke University, I still had a lot of extreme obsessive-compulsive traits, but I had no idea that I was obsessive-compulsive. When I began reading the standard psychiatry textbook on the obsessive-com-

---

* Please see the glossary at the back of this book for definitions of this and other special or technical terms used in the text.

pulsive personality, I carefully studied each page for at least twenty minutes, trying to memorize everything on it.

Two weeks later, I had covered only about forty pages when I read that obsessive-compulsives seldom finish a book. They accumulate a lot of books, but they seldom finish reading one, because they spend so much time poring over each page, trying to memorize everything. Suddenly that information hit me between the eyes. I had to admit that I had all the traits I had been reading about for the past two weeks. That made me so angry that I slammed the book shut. And to this day I haven't finished reading it.

Even though most obsessive-compulsives stress the importance of objective thinking, they often find it hard to take an objective look at themselves. Paul Meier is not the only O-C ever to have difficulty identifying the strengths and weaknesses in his own personality.

WHO IS THE OBSESSIVE-COMPULSIVE?

What is the origin of the term *obsessive-compulsive?* Clinically speaking, an obsession is a particular thought repeated over and over to the point that it is difficult to dislodge from the mind. Such *obsessions* usually result in frequently repeated behavior patterns. Those are known as *compulsions.*

Obsessive-compulsives come in all shapes and sizes and manifest all degrees of obsessive-compulsive behavior. In its extreme, obsessive-compulsive behavior takes the form of agoraphobia (a fear of open places), panic attacks, anxiety attacks, an inability to sleep, and sometimes even difficulty in functioning at all. If the latter occurs, the obsessive-compulsive individual may need to be hospitalized or to receive intensive insight-oriented counseling to discover the root cause of the obsession and the resulting compulsions.

Needless to say, most obsessive-compulsives don't go nearly that far. Examples of relatively normal obsessive-compulsive behavior include the man who frequently pats his hip pocket to see if his wallet is still there, the housewife who calls her husband's office three times to remind him to be sure to get home early to visit with his in-laws, the Sunday school teacher who checks and cross-checks every Scripture reference that will be used in the upcoming lesson, and the football coach who watches the preceding week's game film twenty times, trying to pick up clues to reverse his team's three-game losing streak. And as you can see, obsessive-compulsive behavior isn't necessarily negative.

Dr. Frank Minirth, who admits to being "O-C," has developed a 129-point list describing the major characteristics of the obsessive-compulsive personality trait. Particularly significant is item number 128. It reads, "The obsessive-compulsive likes lists."

The following test of obsessive-compulsive behavior helps us to get to know the O-C a little better.

1. An O-C will figure out a numbering system for almost anything, from wardrobe planning to reading all the research papers in his chosen field. He is especially O-C if he writes research papers.

2. He takes intensive notes in his devotional time. He is especially O-C if he periodically rereads those notes.

3. He takes psychological testing each year just to see if he has grown more obsessive-compulsive.

4. He averaged more than forty pages of class notes for each high school, college, or graduate class. He is especially O-C if he typed up those notes.

5. He always makes it a point to arrive within sixty seconds of the exact time of an appointment. He

is especially O-C if he becomes almost clinically depressed when he is unable to fulfill this commitment.

6. He makes intensive lists of things to do. He is especially O-C if he categorizes his lists on carefully filed 3 x 5 index cards.

7. He feels a desperate need to reorganize his filing system several times a year.

8. He keeps his checkbook balanced—to the penny. If he finds that impossible, he may postpone examining his checkbook figures at all.

9. If he takes a psychological stress test, he will regularly score in the top 5 percentile.

10. He constantly finds himself trying to do two things at once. He dictates letters into a cassette recorder as he drives through rush-hour traffic on a suburban expressway, or writes a research paper on a flight from Tampa to Dallas—at the same time he eats a snack.

11. He finds himself saying, "I'll do it myself, and I'll do it right." If he is blessed with a "Type A personality" as well—with its chronic competitiveness, high achievement orientation, and impatience—he will add, "Right now!"

12. He checks the time more than twice an hour. He is especially O-C if he does this on his day off.

13. He eats while he works. He is especially O-C if he sneaks a granola bar in the elevator, or a Big Mac in rush-hour traffic.

14. He wants to name his children alphabetically from oldest to youngest. He is especially O-C if he wants to alliterate all their names.

If you can identify with a majority of those traits, then the person gazing back at you from the mirror is probably a certified obsessive-compulsive. Now that we have introduced ourselves, let's learn more.

NOTE

1. Please see the glossary at the back of this book for definitions of this and other special or technical terms used in the text.

2
TWO KINDS OF PERFECTIONISTS

In college Harry wanted to participate in almost every campus activity. He played on the basketball and the baseball teams, was active in the campus church, was a member of the college debate team, sang in a choir, took every possible elective course, dated every weekend, and even managed a small business on the side. When Harry finished college, his grade point average hardly reflected his intelligence level. In high school he had been able to keep up his grade level while carrying on numerous outside activities. Too late he discovered that high intelligence alone wasn't enough to ensure his success in college. That would have required that he spend a good deal of time on one goal—his studies.

Julie was in college with Harry. Her grades were good. Whenever Julie worked on an assignment, she'd spend hours on background research. She was never satisfied that she'd done enough. When she typed a paper, it had to be letter perfect. Indeed, typing caused her great anxiety and distraction, for each page had to be error-free. If it wasn't, she'd retype the whole page. She was proud of the fact that she didn't use correction fluid or make erasures on her papers.

But Julie found that her O-C behavior limited her overall college experience. She spent a great deal of her time tidying up her dormitory room and doing her

laundry. She shied away from most of the extracurric-
ular campus activities, and as a result met few people
except at church on Sundays. Even then she barely became acquainted, for she didn't have much experience
in developing close friendships. Julie didn't see the big
picture of how other college activities could develop the
interpersonal skills she would need throughout her
life.

Believe it or not, Julie and Harry were not personality opposites. Instead, both of them had obsessive-
compulsive personality traits, the main one being a
desire to exhibit "perfect" behavior to prove one's personal worth. They both experienced anxiety about not
being accepted, about not being good enough.

Their personalities looked different because they
defined "being good enough" from opposite points of
the spectrum. Harry defined "being good enough"
quantitatively. His biggest worry was that he might
not be participating in enough activities in college. Julie defined "being good enough" qualitatively. Her biggest concern was that she might not be doing any one
thing well enough. Not surprisingly, though they came
from opposite extremes, they shared a difficulty in
dealing with time. Neither one had achieved balance in
the way they regarded and used time.

Put another way, Julie was a *quality* perfectionist
and Harry a *quantity* perfectionist. Julie's obsessive-
compulsive extremes were mixed with some passive-
aggressive behavior. She felt aggression toward doing
what she felt she "ought" to do, so she showed that
aggression passively by dragging her feet when she
worked on a project she thought she should complete.
Because she was also obsessive-compulsive and
thought that everything should be done perfectly, the
two personality traits fed on one another.

Julie took a long time to complete her projects because she could not easily accept her work as good enough to consider any one job completed. In addition, drawing out a project allowed her to act out her negative feelings toward "oughtness" or authority through passivity, that is, by taking longer than necessary to complete what she thought she *should* do.

Harry's Type A behavior consisted of O-C tendencies combined with hysteric or histrionic behavior. He was excessively competitive and highly achievement oriented as long as others could see and appreciate those achievements. He suffered from a chronic sense of time pressure and often was impatient with the pace of life. He wanted to prove to the whole world how good he was at what he did—and how quickly he could do it.

The quantity perfectionist is the one who gives himself twenty things to do in a day, completes nineteen, and then wants to kick himself that night for not getting the twentieth task done. He is usually a firstborn child.

And he does not simply want to do many things. He wants to do many things at once—without concentrating on doing as thorough a job as he might. He wants to please or to win approval from everybody—to have everyone's attention and applause. That can best be done, he thinks, by a flurry of activity, not by doing one thing well. To the Type A obsessive-compulsive, more is better and most is best.

Traditional obsessive-compulsives like Julie usually zero in on accomplishing one thing absolutely perfectly. But they cannot decide what is absolute perfection, so they never consider a project completed, for there might still be some way it could be further perfected. An only child, or the only boy or the only girl in a family, tends to have the combination of O-C and passive-aggressive traits that lean toward this type of quality perfectionism. Such a child is likely to have had perfectionistic parents who did his thinking for him—and who made most of his decisions.

As a consequence, the child has strong obedience-defiance conflicts. Part of him really does want to please the authority figures in his life. So he strives to do what he thinks will please God and his parents and at the same time bring himself personal satisfaction. Yet all the while, he resents the perceived demands of authority figures. So in an unconscious resort to rebellion and vengeance, he acts passively by never actually finishing those tasks he thinks would be pleasing to authority figures.

In Romans 7 the apostle Paul describes such behavior when he says, "I do not understand what I do. For what I want to do I do not do, but what I hate I do. . . . For I have the desire to do what is good, but I cannot carry it out. For what I do is not the good I want to do; no, the evil I do not want to do—this I keep on doing. . . . Who will rescue me from this body of death?" (Romans 7:15; 18b-19; 24b).

THE PROBLEM OF TIME

Obsessive-compulsives tend to take an extreme approach to time. Type A people easily become slaves to the clock. They are constantly looking at their watches, checking calendars, reviewing their daily diaries and lists of things to do, crossing off this and adding that, and endeavoring in every way to cram more and more into less and less time. Evidence that a Type A mentality is flourishing in today's society can be seen in the success of such books as *The One-Minute Manager, The One-Minute Mother,* and *The One-Minute Father.* Each of those books contains simple, easy-to-use principles for dealing with relationships in the workplace or the home. Our purpose is not to criticize such books. They contain much that is useful. But built into the concept of the one-minute person is the principle that it is possible to do more in less time, a major preoccupation of the Type A obsessive-compulsive. Yet even *The One-Minute Father* recognizes that "these . . . methods of personal communication with your children are just a slice of the parenting pie. Being a good parent takes a good deal more than spending a minute now and then with your children."[1]

Can you imagine what it would be like to have a book called *The One-Minute Christian*? Perhaps we should consider such a project. Chapter titles might include "Instant Spirituality," "Fifteen-Second Devotions," "How to Share Your Faith in Half a Minute," "The Forty-Five-Second Prayer Life," "Instant Maturity," "How to See Positive Growth, Grace, and Knowledge in Less Than a Minute." Sounds absurd, doesn't it? But it is not far off the mark as a description of life from the point of view of the Type A obsessive-compulsive struggling to cope in a fast-track society.

Contrast the one-minute mentality with the mindset of the founder of the Procrastinator's Club of America, Les Waas. He believes that the people who fail to relax are the people who die early. So he doesn't mind if you refer to him as the "late" Mr. Waas. In fact, the slogan for his organization is "Procrastinate Now." Procrastinators like Mr. Waas tend to be basically passive-aggressive, and their approach to any deadline is "There's always tomorrow."

Now the basic obsessive-compulsive usually has some passive-aggressive traits. Though he may be

1. Spencer Johnson, *The One-Minute Father* (New York: Morrow, 1983), p. 99.

more conscientious than the basic passive-aggressive person, his personality still leans toward the Procrastinator's Club thinking—that of wanting to rebel against time and deadlines, even reasonable ones.

At the heart of both Harry's and Julie's problems was an inability to focus on what was truly important. Both filled up their days with activity, but neither one used time strategically. Harry ran from activity to activity, and Julie methodically perfected each detail of the tasks she attempted, but neither one achieved a balance of emphasis (focusing one's time strategically) and breadth (participating in a variety of activities) in his total college experience. To do that they would have had to balance the extremes of quality and quantity, something neither one could do.

Jesus and many other biblical figures were able to balance those extremes, however. Jesus demonstrated a significant consciousness of time and of the seasons of the year. He arrived at each destination at just the right time, but He was never rushed, never dilatory. The principles that guided Him can help us achieve a similar balance in our lives.

But before we look at those biblical principles, it will be helpful to deal with certain "road hazards" inherent in the obsessive-compulsive personality. That will be the topic of the next chapter.

3
ROAD HAZARDS OF THE OBSESSIVE-COMPULSIVE

After sitting in on a radio program in which a panel of Christian counselors discussed the obsessive-compulsive personality, a Christian college administrator turned to a friend on the panel and said, "I don't like being an obsessive-compulsive, or whatever it is." Replied his friend, "I'm probably obsessive-obnoxious, and I'm not sure I like it either." During that call-in program, several people had phoned in to voice their dissatisfaction with the obsessive-compulsive personality traits in their lives.

All of those people missed an important point. Though we may not like certain aspects of our personalities, it is important that we accept ourselves. After all, God allowed us to grow up in families where we developed the particular collection of personality strengths and weaknesses we have.

We gain most of our personality traits between the ages of three and six as we learn to relate to our parents and siblings. The obsessive-compulsive personality is usually formed in an oldest child or in the oldest boy or girl. New parents, who often expect more of a small child than he or she can give, drive their first-born to excel early. The child sees that he is more likely to be praised and attended to when he strives for "perfection" than when he simply does what he can with no particular emphasis on perfection. Reaching for perfection to please others becomes a habit early in life.

It is important to remember two overriding principles. First, we need to think of ourselves not with selfish pride or false humility but with sober judgment. God made each of us for a purpose, one that is neither more nor less important than the purpose He has for other individuals. God made us for His glory, and He knew the type of personality each of us would develop. With that in mind, we need to remember the exhortation of the apostle Paul: "Do not think of yourself more highly than you ought, but rather think of yourself with sober judgment [realistically], in accordance with the measure of faith God has given you" (Romans 12:3).

Second, we need to continue in a process of development. As 2 Peter 3:18 puts it, "Grow in the grace and knowledge of our Lord and Savior Jesus Christ." We need to strengthen the strengths we have and work to overcome our weaknesses.

O-C PERSONALITY TRAITS

On first impression, the obsessive-compulsive seems to be a conscientious and dutiful individual, highly motivated toward obedience. He is likely to be a hard worker (usually working too hard), to have a strict conscience, and to be highly motivated. As one hard-working O-C frequently told his children, "Work makes life sweet." The O-C tends to be self-sacrificing and more willing to give up personal gain or desires than some other personality types, which lean toward more selfish behavior.

One of the results of such self-sacrificing behavior is that obsessive-compulsives tend to be extremely successful. Statistically, obsessive-compulsive personalities in mid- to upper-level management positions in American business and industry are outnumbered only by paranoid personality types. Paranoid personalities are afraid of other people's controlling them, so they strive to take control themselves.

The Scottish missionary Eric Liddell, who won a Gold Medal for Britain in the 1924 Olympics for his running, was a classic, dedicated, Christian O-C. He once told an audience, "I believe God made me for a purpose, but He also made me fast. And when I run, I feel His pleasure." He proved that he didn't run to be glorified by others when he sacrificed an opportunity to win an Olympic medal by refusing to run the race on Sunday. His conviction was that Sunday was the Lord's Day, meant only for rest and concentration on the Lord.

A high proportion of the missionaries, Bible college students, pastors, and seminarians we have counseled at the Minirth-Meier Clinic have had a number of obsessive-compulsive personality traits. Many of these individuals were willing to sacrifice lucrative careers to go into the Lord's work. A recent survey of the faculty of a large Christian college also indicated that 80 percent of the teachers considered themselves to be primarily obsessive-compulsive.

Obsessive-compulsives have a strong passion for truth. They tend to be well organized and to handle facts carefully. When they research biblical information they are likely to be careful and accurate—important traits when one is dealing with doctrine and theology.

When taken alone, the obsessive-compulsive traits described above give the impression that the obsessive-compulsive personality type is the most desirable one to have. We know, however, that God didn't make everyone alike. He made us equally important and interdependent on one another. We need, therefore, to recognize the importance of the personable hysteric (or histrionic), the sensitive paranoid, the servant-hearted passive, the highly energetic cyclothimic, and other personalities.

We must also recognize that some negative traits do overshadow the positive aspects of the obsessive-compulsive personality. Most obsessives are aware of those negative traits but tend to deny them, for denial is one of the chief defense mechanisms (reactive behaviors) people employ to cope with the anxiety they would feel if they were fully aware of their sinful or selfish emotions.

ADDITIONAL EXTREME TENDENCIES

The obsessive-compulsive personality is also likely to possess the following extreme characteristics.

PERFECTIONISTIC

A perfectionist has a tendency to expect himself to be perfect all the time. He becomes intensely angry with himself when he demonstrates such imperfections as losing his car keys, forgetting his checkbook, or even failing to keep his checkbook balanced. If an obsessive-compulsive homemaker fails to take care of all her children perfectly, she may become very depressed.

Furthermore, perfectionistic obsessive-compulsives have a tendency to expect perfection from others.

This can create chaos in marital and work relationships, and even may produce another generation of highly perfectionistic, workaholic, obsessive-compulsive children.

DETAIL-ORIENTED

Obsessive-compulsives have a tendency to develop a meticulous concern for detail. They frequently will labor far too hard over a given project. In fact, one obsessive author we know, writing a voluminous book, spent many months writing and rewriting the first three chapters, unable to go on to chapter four, because the first three "just aren't perfect yet." As perfectionists drive themselves to the limit, they are frequently unable or, more accurately, *unwilling* to relax. Obsessive-compulsives become overly concerned about every detail. They are strong in organization but may spend more time getting organized than they spend on just about anything else.

They have a tendency to focus on the future and have a great deal of difficulty relaxing and enjoying life in the present. Obsessives are the kind of individuals who, when eating a hot fudge sundae save what they consider the best part, the maraschino cherry on top of the whipped cream, for last. Or, after considering the amount of number-two red dye contained in that topping, they refuse to eat the cherry at all!

PROJECT-DIRECTED

Obsessive-compulsives tend to focus on projects rather than on people. This is undergirded by an orientation toward facts rather than feelings. Psychiatric research has long demonstrated that the left side of the human brain is used for processing factual or logical data. The right side is used for more creative thinking as well as emotional or relational thought. Obsessive-compulsives tend to rely primarily on the data-oriented part of their thinking. In fact, obsessives have a strong tendency to deny most emotional feelings or responses, even though they are frequently dominated by strong, underlying emotions. You might say that the obsessive *feels* with his mind.

Furthermore, obsessive-compulsives have a tendency to criticize themselves and others for being less than perfect. Coupled with that is a motivation toward control—of self, circumstances, personal environment, and others. All Christians tend to feel inferior at some time and try to compensate for those feelings of inferiority. On the part of the obsessive-compulsive, those inferiority feelings lead to power struggles because of their strong motivation to be in control. Both internal and interpersonal conflicts are often the result.

Members of a large division of a Fortune 500 company had a party in honor of their vice-president, not to celebrate his retirement or even his hiring, but his being fired. The vice-president was strongly control-oriented. Throughout his division, he insisted on personally supervising and approving even the simplest decisions, such as which office supplies the secretaries purchased and from which vendors they ordered them.

Many workaholic obsessive-compulsives have what might well be described as a "Martha complex." During Jesus' last week on earth, Martha opened her home to Jesus. Mary, Martha's sister, sat and listened to Jesus as Martha busied herself preparing a meal. Martha displayed numerous obsessive-compulsive traits in her first recorded utterance to Jesus, "Lord, don't you care that my sister has left me to do the work by myself? Tell her to help me!" (Luke 10:40).

The traits exposed in that one statement revealed that Martha:

- considered the *project* of having the Savior for dinner more important than acknowledging the *Person* of Jesus Christ.
- labored far too hard over the project.
- would not or could not relax and enjoy the Lord's presence.
- preferred working to anything else.
- was critical of her sister, Mary (for not helping her), and even of Jesus (for not having encouraged Mary to help her).
- was motivated to control Mary as well as Jesus (to help her control Mary).
- took action that would likely lead to interpersonal conflicts.

Jesus' reply to Martha put the differing outlooks of the two sisters into proper perspective, although what He said was something that an obsessive-compulsive would find disagreeable, even when the words were from Jesus Himself.

> Martha, Martha, . . . you are worried and upset [tied up in knots, distracted] about many things, but only one thing is needed. Mary has chosen what is better [relating personally with others, particularly with Jesus], and it will not be taken away from her. [Luke 10:41]

DIRT-OBSESSED

The obsessive-compulsive's concern with dirt gives us a candid look at perfectionism. The key question is, how clean is clean enough? As a young boy, one of the authors was taught by his mother how to wash dishes.

He never enjoyed the chore, partly because he never knew how clean was clean enough, and partly because his mother was somewhat obsessive-compulsive herself. She always insisted that the dishes be carefully scrubbed in scalding water, rinsed in hot water to remove all germs, then rinsed again in cold water to remove all traces and residue of soap (which might have caused diarrhea). Finally, the dishes needed to be carefully dried and put away.

While he did the dishes, this particular author wrestled with the question, how hot does the water have to be and for how long must the dishes be immersed in it to kill every single germ? In fact, can that be done? Is it worth the trouble? What if one germ slips through? The result of this kind of obsession is obvious: childhood training that spawns such fearful thoughts can cause children to develop obsessive-compulsive personality problems.

Dirt in other areas of life—personal hygiene, housekeeping, laundry—is often an obsession. "Cleanliness is next to godliness" is the maxim that spells disaster for some obsessive-compulsives. To them, perfect cleanliness can mean the next best thing to perfection itself. It becomes a substitute for washing one's sins or imperfections away so that one can be more perfect and acceptable.

MONEY-FOCUSED

The obsessive-compulsive tends to be conservative, which can be a positive trait; however, this particular characteristic is often taken to the extreme. Because of a strong need to feel secure and in control, obsessives tend to be strongly money-oriented. In fact, many obsessive-compulsive church treasurers will treat church funds like their own, rather than the

Lord's. They will not only exercise the conscientious stewardship demanded of a person serving in that position but will treat any expenditures, even those for benevolent purposes, as a personal affront, justifying such an attitude in the name of financial conservatism.

At times, an obsessive-compulsive husband may deeply resent the needs of his wife to spend money on their children, a new hairdo, a dress, or on other personal expenses because of his strong desire to save that money for the future.

TEMPTATIONS OF THE O-C

Like every other Christian, the obsessive-compulsive has an "old nature" that manifests itself in sinful or selfish behavior. With more than five billion people on planet earth, each of us feels insignificant and inferior to some extent. We try to compensate for those feelings through selfish, sinful, or inappropriate behavior patterns. Three such behavior patterns outlined for us in 1 John 2:13-15 are the lust of the flesh—*sexual and other physical enticements;* the lust of the eyes—*materialism,* or preoccupation with money and material things; and the pride of life—*power struggles,* or a desire to control, dominate, or be more prominent than other people.

Obsessives can fall into sexual temptation, especially because of their tendency to deny emotions, their own sexuality, or their need for emotional intimacy. However, they tend to be tempted primarily in two other areas—materialism and power struggles.

MATERIALISM

Because of their preoccupation with money, obsessives can become very materialistic. Frequently, their materialistic behaviors are hidden under the guise of

"saving for the future." Sometimes obsessive-compulsives refuse to give to God or to others because of their
strong drive to build up personal security by saving.
That kind of behavior was demonstrated by the farmer
who tore down his barns to build bigger ones, a pattern condemned as foolish by the Lord Jesus Christ.
The possession of money is not wrong, but as Paul
pointed out to Timothy, the *love* of money is the root of
all kinds of evil. While the love of money is obvious and
overt in other personalities, it may be more subtle in
the obsessive-compulsive and therefore more difficult
to deal with.

POWER STRUGGLES

A second major area of temptation, and perhaps
the most crucial for Christian obsessive-compulsives,
is the desire for power, or the "pride of life." Because
they themselves usually have experienced a great deal
of conditional love (a concept we will deal with later),
obsessive-compulsives tend to approach others with
the same attitude. As one obsessive-compulsive put it,
"I love my fellow workers unconditionally, but they just
don't measure up to my performance standards." That
same person later acknowledged that these personal
feelings were at the root of several intense, on-the-job
conflicts in his Christian working environment.

The intensely competitive nature of obsessive-
compulsives frequently makes them successful in their
work. Yet the kind of success they achieve is often
worldly success in contrast to the kind of success that
Jesus commends in Luke 22:25-26:

> Jesus said to them, "The kings of the Gentiles
> lord it over them; and those who exercise authority
> over them call themselves Benefactors. But you are
> not to be like that. Instead, the greatest among you

should be like the youngest, and the one who rules like the one who serves."

It is important for the obsessive-compulsive to work at avoiding inappropriate obsessive behavior patterns, especially crucial ones such as workaholism, materialism, power struggles, and self-critical, perfectionistic behavior. How to do that will be explored later.

Now that we see how obsessive-compulsives behave, let's look at how they think and feel.

4
IS MY THINKING STRAIGHT?

Obsessive-compulsive personalities usually have strong mental capacities and seem to be fact-oriented. They are ideal for jobs that demand an ability to master a number of facts. Good researchers, accountants, computer programmers, airline pilots, air traffic controllers, nurses, doctors, pastors, theologians, business administrators, managers, and many other professional workers usually include numerous balanced obsessive-compulsive individuals who utilize factual, organizational, and work-ethic strengths.

However, although obsessives are thinkers, they do not always think accurately. The following are a sampling of some irrational beliefs held by Type A obsessive-compulsives.

TYPE A OBSESSIVE-COMPULSIVE THINKING

1. *Quantity of output is more important than quality of output.* The major emphasis of Type A obsessive-compulsives is to "churn out" a lot of work. For instance, three highly productive obsessive-compulsives decided to form a "book of the month" club. They weren't going to read a book each month, however; they intended to *write* a book each month, in addition to their already busy schedules and other demands.

Every day Joe makes lists of fifteen to twenty things to do. He feels motivated to check off his list daily, even if the items are poorly or sloppily done. It doesn't bother him if they're not done well, but it does bother him if they are not checked off. But for the Christian, excellence ought not to be simply a matter of checking off items on a list. It involves establishing a balance between quality and quantity, even as we recognize that we are not perfect in either category. Instead, success means giving our best in any given situation.

2. *Faster is always better.* Many obsessives' lives are like a treadmill moving faster and faster. And, somehow, the charge of adrenalin from life in the fast lane motivates them to work even more rapidly. Though the passive-aggressive O-C personality tends to become slower and slower under pressure, the Type A obsessive works faster, talks faster, and even tries to think faster. Unfortunately, working faster doesn't always produce a better product. In fact, faster can create disaster.

Consider Wayne. Wayne works in a factory that rebuilds spark plugs. Although he was already doing a fine job reaching his assigned quota, he wanted to turn out more rebuilt spark plugs than the other workers. But in the process of working faster, he ruined an entire batch of plugs and cost the company a large sum of money. As a result, he was reprimanded for working *too* fast. Life is like freeway driving. We shouldn't be moving so fast or so slow that we're out of sync with the rest of the traffic.

3. *Horrible disaster will occur if deadlines are not met.* A highly successful Christian radio professional became physically ill when through a number of unavoidable circumstances, including equipment failure, a documentary missed a preparation deadline.

Such feelings would have been perfectly understandable, except that in this case the deadline missed was seventy-two hours before the documentary was scheduled to be broadcast. In the October 19, 1976, *Family Health Magazine*, psychologist Leonard Cammer asks, "What about your punctuality? Mostly, it serves you in good stead, but can you allow yourself to be five or ten minutes late when it really would make no difference? Do you panic at the very thought?"

Here is one O-C who learned the benefits of procrastination. Horace, a pastor, learned of a conflict in his church. His initial reaction was to attempt to gather all the people involved in the conflict in his office that same day. Because of his schedule, however, he was unable to do that. In the meantime, those directly involved in the problem got together and resolved it, probably much more adequately than if the pastor had tried to wade into it. A lesson that many of us need to learn is that meeting deadlines is far less important than dealing with people, issues, or even taking time out. A good biblical example of that is Jesus' timing regarding the death of Lazarus and His arrival in Bethany. According to Lazarus' family, Jesus was several days late; yet in reality He was exactly on time. Another example is Mark 6:30 where we find Jesus and His disciples taking time out. (See the Minirth-Meier booklet *Taking Time Out*, published by Moody Press.)

Paul Meier likes to give this advice to obsessive-compulsives: Never do today what you can put off till tomorrow.

4. *Winning or losing a competition is a reflection of my worth as a human being.* In American society professional sports, business, and industry have produced a "win at all cost" mentality. Seminars are available to aid individuals in "winning" the game of life, which usually means successfully competing with oth-

ers. College football fans from various universities discuss the relative merits of their favorite team and which team will be crowned the national champion. In professional sports the Super Bowl, the World Series, and the NBA playoff finals settle the same question. However, in any competition there is always one winner—and many losers. Unfortunately, we have somehow developed a connection that links personal worth to winning. Thus, when we lose, we feel horrible. A magazine article describes a twenty-game-winning major league pitcher as unable to accept losing and feeling totally worthless whenever it happened.

For the Christian, the goal is to win God's approval in the race of life (1 Corinthians 9).

5. *I am only as good as my accomplishments.* This is closely linked with the previous belief. One way of spotting Type A obsessive-compulsive behavior, particularly the workaholic kind, is to check your conversation. Do you spend a lot of time talking about your accomplishments? (You may not be the best judge of this—so check with your wife or husband, your children, your business associates, or other professionals with whom you interact.) Frequently, we focus on our accomplishments because we feel we are *only as good as our achievements.* However, for Christians, personal worth is rooted in our *position* in Jesus Christ, not in our performance. It is irrational for the Christian to feel so competitive or achievement oriented that self-worth becomes linked to personal accomplishments. Nor will an endless string of achievements insure that we will like ourselves. Usually, a list of accomplishments simply produces either an appropriate response —thanking God for the positive things He allows me to achieve, while giving Him the glory—or an inappropriate response—feeling that I am really special because of what I achieve, or worthless because of my

inability to achieve. These feelings lead to another irrational belief.

6. *Nonachievement-oriented activities are a waste of time.* Why do the spouses of Type A obsessive-compulsive workaholics frequently complain that they are ignored when it comes to personal conversation? Why do their children often feel conditionally loved or, worse, neglected? Why do Type A's look for excuses to work overtime, bring work home from the office, and try to do three or four things at once? Because of the irrational conviction that nonachievement-oriented activities are just a waste of time. There is no question that wasting time is a sin, but it is probably not as great a sin as most Type A O-Cs assume. Furthermore, the list of activities considered time-wasters by Type A O-Cs is a lot longer than the lists other personality types would create. Even Jesus told His overworked disciples, "Come with me by yourselves to a quiet place and get some rest" (Mark 6:31). Although rest is an activity considered a time-waster by many Type A O-Cs, there is positive value to time away from the productive mind-set.

In fact, God places a premium on certain nonachievement-oriented activities such as relationships, rest, and even waiting. Some time ago a friend challenged one of the authors to study the concept of waiting in Scripture. After some procrastination, the study was completed. It proved to be an insightful study, as the author learned the value of waiting and discovered several benefits individuals in Scripture received by heeding instructions to wait.

7. *I can have complete control over my life if I only try hard enough.* The obsessive-compulsive is often convinced, without rational foundation, that just a little more effort will give him or her complete control

over circumstances, self, and even others. To the obsessive-compulsive, nothing seems worse than "losing control." Obsessive-compulsives have been known to become extremely angry and depressed when placed in emotional circumstances that bring tears. In traffic, Type A obsessives sometimes feel they can make all the traffic lights if they just drive hard and fast enough. Being put on hold on the telephone, being caught in a traffic jam, spending time circling a busy airport—those kinds of uncontrollable situations make life miserable for the Type A obsessive-compulsive. A frequent corollary to this for the Type A is the thought that speeding up the pace of his activities is the best way to keep or regain control.

The obsessive-compulsive needs constantly to remind himself that personal effort is always secondary to utilizing God's resources. The best example of that is the apostle Paul in 2 Corinthians 12. No amount of personal effort could remove his thorn in the flesh. In that situation God explained to Paul that His strength was being perfected in Paul's weakness. Read Isaiah 40, which is another classic example of those who renew their strength by waiting on the Lord. The truth is that God is the only One who really can or should be in control. So why should we worry about being in control in life? We can't be.

8. *Being perfectionistic is the best way to insure high quality achievements.* A successful, obsessive-compulsive medical doctor had always made straight A's throughout high school and college. When he reached medical school, suddenly he found himself to be just one of the average students, since all the rest of the medical students were also the "cream of the crop" in their high schools and colleges. To assure himself of quality achievements, this doctor became increasingly perfectionistic and, in the process, became highly crit-

ical of himself and others. His marriage relationship became strained, and his friends began to avoid him. He expected perfection of himself and of others. He had not reconciled himself to the fact that none of us is perfect. Only Jesus Christ reached sinless perfection. Not even the apostle Paul, who, prior to his conversion, probably was extremely obsessive-compulsive as a "Pharisee of the Pharisees," was perfect.

Often, relaxing perfectionistic standards leads to greater excellence and more successful results than perfectionism does. On one of our radio programs Texas Rangers catcher Jeff Sundberg told of pushing himself and trying harder but being less successful at the plate. But his batting average improved dramatically after his batting coach encouraged him to relax and have fun at the plate.

The bumper sticker on one reformed obsessive-compulsive's car reads, "Christians aren't perfect, just forgiven." Being perfectionistic only underscores how far we can fall. We all fall short of perfection, which leads to feelings of anger and depression in the Type A obsessive.

9. *Openly expressing my anger and hostility makes other people pay for getting in my way.* Although many Christian Type A obsessives would not admit to such thoughts, they tend to couch them in terms of "appropriate" confrontation. "I believe in taking a strong stand for my convictions." "I believe in confronting people when they need to be confronted." One young obsessive-compulsive pastor was involved in three church splits before somebody finally communicated to him that it wasn't his "biblical confrontation" of sin in the lives of others or their personal shortcomings that was causing the problems. Rather, it was his own underlying anger and hostility that created the series of tragic rifts.

The proper alternative to expressing anger is to acknowledge and confront it. The next step is to turn the issue of vengeance over to God, particularly because Scripture teaches us to do so. Three times in the New Testament we are instructed that God is to be in charge of vengeance (Romans 12; 1 Thessalonians 5; 1 Peter 3). We must place it in His hands.

What we discover as we consider this facet of the Type A obsessive-compulsive is that, although he generally has superior thinking capabilities, he is susceptible to numerous irrational thoughts. Those thoughts are related to some very strong underlying emotions, ones the obsessive-compulsive refuses to acknowledge but which nonetheless play a key role in his or her life. They will be discussed in the next chapter.

5
FACING MY FEELINGS

This chapter is being written while seated in a DC-9 aircraft on a Monday morning against the beautiful mountain backdrop of Colorado Springs. However, I shouldn't be here. This aircraft was scheduled to leave nearly two hours earlier than it did. First, we experienced a fog delay. A half hour later, while we were taxiing into position for takeoff, the pilot ran the aircraft off the edge of the runway. We were stuck in the mud for almost two hours. Finally, the plane was pulled from the mud, restored to the runway, and readied for takeoff. During the delay the pilot consoled us over the intercom, "I feel terrible about this. It is an awful way to begin a Monday morning. I know most of you have tight schedules and connecting flights to make."

How did the passengers feel? Most were fairly good-natured, but several voiced anger over fouled-up flight schedules and connections. Others were fearful of missing important meetings or appointments. And underlying several of the conversations with flight attendants were feelings of guilt for expressing those emotions of anger and fear. It was obvious that many of those passengers had a number of obsessive-compulsive traits.

Although most obsessive-compulsives have strong feelings, they do not like to feel. They would much rather think. They keep their emotions hidden from others and, if possible, from themselves. As a result, obsessive-compulsives may seem cold and indifferent.

Rick, a highly successful senior pastor of a large evangelical church, was known to his congregation as a gifted communicator and a capable administrator. Yet many people considered him to be cold in his personal relationships, unfeeling, and unable to relate to the emotional expressions of others. Speaking to a member of our counseling staff, he conceded that he was more interested in facts than in feelings. And even though he recognized the need for hospital visitation, counseling, and other people-oriented aspects of ministry, he strongly preferred to study in his office with the door closed while his secretary screened personal calls and visits.

EMOTIONS

What emotions do most obsessive-compulsives actually feel? Let's examine some typical O-C emotions and how they deal with them.

ANGER

According to a number of authorities, a primary emotion of obsessives is anger. Many obsessive-compulsives had strong, dominant parents who demanded unquestioning obedience and forbade their children to express anger, classifying such as tantamount to rebellion. Thus, in early life the obsessive-compulsive developed a struggle between obedience and defiance.

Outwardly, obsessives are usually extremely compliant, so we know that the pull of obedience usually wins. Occasionally, however, defiance wins. When obsessives submit or comply, that obedience usually creates feelings of strong anger, sometimes even rage.

As one obsessive-compulsive housewife put it, "Both
my parents expected me always to do exactly what they
said. I usually did, but underneath I seethed."

When asked, "Did you ever decide not to comply
with their wishes?" her reply was, "Seldom. I was
scared to death whenever I didn't do what they said."

FEAR

On the rare occasions when obsessives allow defiance to win out over their inclination toward obedience, the act of defiance will later lead to even stronger
feelings of fear of authority. Actually that defiance is
fear of parental authority left over from childhood. Although obsessive-compulsives do not like to admit it,
they are frequently dominated by powerful emotions of
intense anger or fear. Their fears tend to lead to perfectionistic traits and to future compliance, whereas their
feelings of anger or rage often lead to nonperfectionist-
ic traits and a present refusal to comply.

Thus, while obsessive-compulsives tend to be conscientious in most areas of their lives, they usually
have a few areas in which they tend to be extremely
negligent. For example, one obsessive-compulsive who
was always punctual, orderly, and neat, frequently
misplaced his keys. An obsessive-compulsive housewife who managed two children, a husband's ministry
career, and a college-level computer course successfully, nonetheless found it extremely difficult to maintain
any semblance of neatness in her home. Obsessive-
compulsives often tend to be characterized by oppos-
ing traits that arise from their mixed feelings.

Just what does the obsessive-compulsive fear? He
fears:

Dependency. He prefers relationships in which he
is in control and others are dependent on him.

Close relationships. Close relationships demand emotional vulnerability or dependency, feelings that are unthinkable and highly undesirable to the obsessive-compulsive.

Loss of control. Being in control of himself and having control over his circumstances is of extreme importance to the O-C. He feels helpless and fears those feelings of helplessness whenever he loses control. The more he experiences feelings of powerlessness, the more an obsessive under stress wants to "do something about it," even when the appropriate course of action may be to "wait on the Lord."

GUILT

Related to anger and fear are the feelings of guilt experienced by most obsessive-compulsives. While guilt is a valid emotion created by the Holy Spirit to warn us when we are wrong, we fallen human beings tend to experience one of two extremes of this emotion. Self-centered, sociopathic personalities (aspects of which all of us are born with to some degree) tend to minimize or ignore feelings of guilt while persisting in selfish or sociopathic behavior that fulfills the biblical description of having "consciences seared with a hot iron." They seldom feel guilty, even when they should.

On the other hand, some Christians, because of strict upbringings and exposure to legalistic teaching, feel guilty about almost anything. For example, one of the authors was raised in a strict home where reading a newspaper was not allowed on Sunday. It took years for him to feel comfortable when sitting down to scan the front page, the sports section, or even the comics, not because any Scripture says, "Thou shalt not peruse the Sunday paper," but because of a combination of parental upbringing and inappropriate guilt.

Many obsessive-compulsives are plagued by an overly strict conscience, one that causes continued feelings of guilt and lack of forgiveness long after a failure. For example, a conscientious college student was cheating in school primarily because of years of being unsuccessful and parental disapproval. When he was caught and confronted with his misconduct, he confessed, both to God and to the school authorities. During the balance of his college career, he maintained a "clean slate." However, feelings of guilt and even depression over the incident continued to plague him years later, hampering his efforts to minister to others. The problem was not with God's forgiveness or with the student's refusal to acknowledge his sin. Like many of his obsessive-compulsive colleagues, the student had admitted his failure to live up to God's absolute standard of perfection and had accepted God's forgiveness, yet he could not forgive himself or quiet his hyperactive conscience.

Because of the tendency to deny feelings or to turn them inward, O-C's tend to experience a greater degree of depression than almost any other personality type.

Another kind of obsessive-compulsive, however, has a tendency to hold in feelings of anger and then occasionally ventilate them, often in hostile, aggressive, or inappropriate ways. In fact, as one obsessive-compulsive businessman put it, "It is much easier for me to express myself when I am feeling angry with my wife than when I want to express warmth." Through intensive counseling he discovered the reason for that. He was extremely fearful of becoming emotionally close or dependent and used anger to maintain what he considered to be a safe distance in his relationships.

Obsessive-compulsives become angry with others who affect or limit their ability to be "perfect," with themselves for their own imperfections, and perhaps even angry at their own feelings. They may be angry with God for allowing circumstances to prove their imperfections.

A classic biblical example of an obsessive outburst of sinful and inappropriate behavior is the incident in Numbers 20:2-13, where Moses struck the rock against God's instructions. Although God had provided water for Israel through a similar incident in the past (in which Moses followed God's instructions to the letter by smiting the rock once), under the stress of Israel's constant carping and complaining, Moses exhibited the underlying anger of a normally obedient O-C that came boiling to the top. God said to Moses, "Speak to the rock." But Moses' anger was overflowing. "Listen, you rebels, must we bring you water out of this rock?" (v. 10) He then *struck* (but did not speak to) the rock— twice.

In this incident Moses exhibited all three primary emotions of an obsessive-compulsive:

- *anger*—with the Israelites, with God, with himself, and with the circumstances
- *fear*—of loss of control or of being unable to "produce" (seen in the statement "Must we bring you water?")
- *guilt*—when God confronted him (God disciplined Moses by forbidding him to enter the Promised Land)

DEFENSE MECHANISMS

Frequently, the obsessive-compulsive copes with his feelings by using defense mechanisms. Defense mechanisms are the automatic and subconscious ways we respond to conflict or frustration. In essence, they are ways in which we deceive ourselves to avoid facing our true desires, emotions, and motives.

Two verses of Scripture illustrate this point. The first is Proverbs 21:2, "All a man's ways seem right to him, but the Lord weighs the heart." That shows how commonly we exercise self-righteousness to justify things we do, even when our motives are improper.

The second verse is Jeremiah 17:9, "The heart is deceitful above all things, and desperately wicked" (KJV*). We consider this verse to be the cornerstone of Christian counseling. Obviously, the more we become aware of the truth about ourselves, the better we will be able to engage in Christlike, or biblical, thinking, feeling, and behavior. Although every individual practices defense mechanisms many times each day, certain defenses are most common to obsessive-compulsives. Let's examine these mechanisms.

DENIAL

An individual using this defense mechanism denies access to consciousness of thoughts, feelings, or motives. Although denial is most commonly seen in histrionic or hysteric (outwardly emotional, attention-seeking) personalities, obsessives frequently practice denial regarding emotions such as anger or fear. For example, one obsessive-compulsive pastor was experiencing marital conflict, yet insisted that he had never been angry with his wife. What he meant was that he had never allowed himself to get in touch with his feelings of anger—feelings that in many instances were already evident to his wife.

* King James Version.

INTELLECTUALIZATION

Individuals who intellectualize frequently develop strong inferiority feelings. Yet they cover those feelings by attempting to impress others, using extensive philosophical discussion, technical jargon, and intellectual vocabulary. We knew a seminary student who spent hours in the coffee shop discussing philosophical and theological issues and debating obscure concepts. But in spite of all that discussion, he never got in touch with his feelings.

ISOLATION

The individual who practices isolation separates or isolates unacceptable feelings from his conscious awareness. This is one of the more common ways obsessives deal with anger, particularly those who have been taught that all anger is sin. At times, individuals who believe feelings of greed or lust are totally unacceptable isolate those emotions in spite of the fact that most normal people do experience them from time to time.

REACTION FORMATION

Often found with isolation, reaction formation is adopting attitudes or actions that are the exact opposite of those conscious or unconscious impulses we experience. An example would be a television evangelist who preaches long sermons against materialism but secretly holds large bank accounts. Or a youth pastor who has strict and complex rules forbidding the young people in his church to have any physical contact with the opposite sex, but who secretly reads pornographic magazines and views sexually explicit movies.

PHARISEEISM

Those who practice phariseeism become increasingly self-righteous. The Pharisee (in Luke 18) thanked God that he was not as others—robbers, evildoers, adulterers—and carefully maintained a list of dos and don'ts, tailor-made to his personal preferences and designed to maintain his own personal selfishness, hostility, and anger. Those who practice phariseeism frequently regard anyone less legalistic than themselves as worldly or even diabolical. They make a great show of religious ritual to cover up their inappropriate emotions. One pharisaical preacher was exhorting his flock not to engage in the evils of drinking. "I am the temple of the Holy Spirit," he admonished with a sweeping gesture of his arm, which caused a hidden package of cigarettes to fall from his pocket in full view of his astonished congregation.

MAGICAL THINKING

Magical thinking is a defense mechanism by which individuals compensate for feelings of inferiority by fooling themselves into thinking they have subtle supernatural powers. This tends to be present to a greater degree in obsessive-compulsive adults and young children than in other groups of people. It is extreme in those suffering from schizophrenia but manifests itself more mildly in obsessives.

One immature Christian obsessive was trying to decide whether to marry the girl he was dating or begin dating another girl. Deciding to seek "God's will" by using a form of magical thinking, he opened his Bible and came across a verse that read, "He taketh away the first, that he may establish the second" (Hebrews 10:9). Convinced that he had found God's clear direction, he broke off his relationship with the first young lady and married the second. Whatever God's will regarding the marriage, the young man had clearly violated the rules for biblical interpretation in his use of that verse.

Magical thinking frequently leads to guilt in obsessives who become angry at friends or relatives but later experience some tragedy. One young obsessive housewife had shouted over the telephone at her mother the day before her mother suffered an automobile accident. Her mother later died of the resulting injuries. It took months of intensive therapy to help that obsessive-compulsive individual recover from her magical thinking that left her believing that she had in some way caused the mishap.

UNDOING

Undoing is the unhealthy side of appropriate restitution, that is, offering an apology or attempting to right specific wrongs we have done to others. Obsessives and others who practice undoing try to perform positive verbal communication or benevolent acts, attempting to counter other negative acts. The problem is that they do that without acknowledging the wrong deeds, as if they had never made the errors.

One example of undoing was a Christian lady who frequently criticized the members of her women's Bible study group behind their backs. However, when she was with them, she was warm, effusive, and outgoing in her praise and encouragement—almost to excess. Because she considered herself to be a highly encouraging and positive individual, she managed to use that undoing as a means of escaping personal awareness of her sinful gossip and criticism. Whether with respect to inappropriate thinking or undesirable emotions, obsessive-compulsives find it extremely painful to face the truth.

Some secular psychologists encourage the use of defense mechanisms to "prevent insanity." However, a more biblical alternative for mental health is to experience the forgiveness from sin that results from the new birth in Christ, and to allow the Word of God to progressively conform us to Christ as we study, meditate, and apply it to our sinful thought patterns, emotions, and motives.

Jesus pointed out to a group of obsessives, "You will know the truth, and the truth will set you free" (John 8:32). Unfortunately, the response of those highly obsessive Pharisees was denial. "We are Abraham's descendants and have never been slaves of anyone" (v. 33).

Though it may be painful to discover the truth about our emotions, such as guilt, fear, and anger, as well as about our dualistic and inappropriate thinking, it is important for us to progressively give up our defense mechanisms in order to become emotionally and spiritually healthy.

6
HOW DID I GET THIS WAY?

Recently one of us was speaking at a conference in a Western state. During the conference this author stayed in the home of a staff member of a parachurch organization. Following the service one evening his hostess stated rather strongly, "I am really not sure I agree with all of what you said about obsessive-compulsive behavior or workaholism. In fact, I don't like it."

"Really?" the author replied. "Tell me why."

"I just think those things don't apply to me."

"Tell me a little about yourself," the speaker replied.

"Well, I am certainly not obsessive-compulsive or a workaholic," she said. "However, my dad certainly was. He was an extremely critical, highly demanding, hardworking businessman, and he expected a lot out of us. In fact, I decided early in life that I would make it a point not to be at all like my father."

It's not hard to imagine the direction the conversation took. Within half an hour the housewife reluctantly began to admit that she had a number of obsessive-compulsive personality traits—characteristics she had sought to suppress or deny for years. Finally, she threw up her hands. "The reason I didn't like what you were saying is that it described me to a 'T.' I must have caught my father's obsessive-compulsive behavior after all."

However, being an obsessive-compulsive is not a "caught" behavior. And there is no evidence that O-C traits are hereditary. Psychological studies indicate that the primary factor is one's early environment. Many of those studies indicate that the majority of our personality traits are formed prior to our sixth birthday and certainly by the time one becomes a teenager.

Most individuals with a large number of obsessive-compulsive traits have parents who were also obsessive. A person is especially likely to become O-C if the parent of the opposite sex was extremely strict, demanded complete devotion and total obedience, and gave a minimal amount of attention—love, affection, hugs, or positive strokes. To such a parent, everything was either black or white. The child was either a success or a failure. So the child felt accepted on a conditional basis. That conditional love led to the child's need to achieve or to perform to get the parent's approval.

As one highly motivated obsessive-compulsive told her counselor, "Dad was very successful in his business, but he wasn't very good at relating to my mother or to us children. He always expected us to be the best, but he never seemed to think that we could do anything. Whether it was chores around the house, helping him with his business, or doing things at school, we had to be perfect." When asked if her father had ever told her that he loved her, her quick reply was, "No, never. Not until I was grown and out of the house."

"Did he give you lots of hugs when you were growing up?"

"No, he wasn't affectionate at all."

This daughter, like many obsessive-compulsives, attempted superhuman achievements to try to overcome her feelings of uncertainty that conditional love had produced.

Describing the workaholic, obsessive-compulsive father in the *Wall Street Journal* (April 6, 1981), Sanford L. Jacobs writes, "He gets home long after the children have eaten. She used to eat with them but now she waits for her husband. Usually the children have gone to bed by then. One child asked recently, 'Isn't daddy going to be home again tonight?'" Two possible consequences of obsessive-compulsive, workaholic behavior in parents are: (1) a child acts out and tells the parent to "buzz off," and (2) the oldest child develops an intense motivation to strive after achievements to try to win the workaholic or obsessive-compulsive parent's approval.

The great majority of obsessive-compulsives are workaholics, and most workaholics have a large number of obsessive-compulsive personality traits.

Type A behavior patterns also fit many obsessive-compulsive workaholics. They exhibit the following characteristics:

1. *High competitiveness.* Everything Type A's do becomes competition, even in relationships. That sometimes causes them to encourage competitiveness in their children. As a result, a Type A workaholic usually encourages his children to strive after achievements, rather than accepting them for who they are. Frequently, spouses compete with each other, sabotaging meaningful communication and peaceful coexistence in the home. Their competitiveness also affects their job circumstances and even their recreational activities.

2. *Excessive striving for achievement.* Involve a Type A obsessive-compulsive in conversation, and soon the subject becomes his or her latest project or list of achievements—either those already accomplished or those he is about to perform. He or she usually experiences an inability to say no. Thus, as time passes, the list of things to do generally grows longer rather than shorter.

3. *Impatience or hurry sickness.* Type A obsessive-compulsives despise waiting for elevators. They would much rather take the stairs, even if there are twenty flights. They can't stand being placed on hold on the telephone, and traffic tie-ups sometimes leave them feeling physically ill. As one Type A person described it, "For me and others like me, life probably consists of three words: *hurry, worry,* and *bury.*" A consequence of this trait is that because of his schedule, the Type A workaholic generally finds it hard to spend more than a few minutes in passing with his children. Also time spent with children is generally relational rather than task-oriented, so it is even more difficult for him to make the effort to be with them. Since Type A workaholics frequently can't say no to anyone, they usually end up saying no to their family by default. Such behavior patterns led to the writing of the book *When I Relax I Feel Guilty.*

4. *Aroused anger and hostility.* When asked whether their fathers gave them more positive or negative verbal feedback and reinforcement, a group of pastors responded almost unanimously that they received 75 to 90 percent negative feedback. As one of them put it, "My dad was always blowing his stack at me. He came home with all this anger from work and took it out on us kids, especially me, since I was the oldest."

Another common characteristic of the obsessive-compulsive is that he gives himself and others a highly disproportionate number of "should," "ought," or "must" messages. Although clear parental direction is extremely important, constantly communicating "shoulds," "oughts," or "musts" to our children leads them to believe that if they don't perform, they aren't worthy. That message, reinforced throughout childhood, produces many second-generation obsessive-compulsives. A number of psychological studies reveal the following list of traits found in parents of obsessive-compulsives:

- *They spend a great amount of time talking to their children but very little time listening.* Most of their talk centers on commands, instructions, criticisms, and the previously discussed "should" messages.
- *Obsessive-compulsive parents have a tendency to expect perfect manners, even at an early age.* One particularly obsessive-compulsive couple pushed their children into church each Sunday and seated them in descending order from the oldest to the youngest and wouldn't allow even a wiggle out of the two-year-old. Obsessive-compulsive parents don't tolerate mistakes, not even a small amount of spilled milk.
- *Obsessive-compulsives tend to be extremely critical of other people, especially in front of their children.* Many of them practice snobbery, and even Christian O-Cs tend to put down others with whom they come in contact. By the same token, friends of obsessive-compulsives are often introverts and seldom allow their children to interact openly with other people.
- *Obsessive-compulsive parents have a tendency to emphasize the letter of the law, to the extent of practicing phariseeism.* Emphasizing the Victorian ethic, they tend to communicate to their children the view that high moral standards demonstrate personal superiority and can even contribute toward

earning one's way to heaven, a notion obviously contrary to the gospel of God's grace. Such an emphasis
frequently results in obsessive Christians who feel
insecure in their relationship with Christ. However,
despite personal rigidity and "no exception" rules,
obsessive-compulsive parents frequently avoid any
serious personal commitment to God. Their commitment is on the surface.

- *Obsessive-compulsive parents are usually extremely critical of the material convictions of the child's
grandparents, which frequently they characterize
as miserly.* The grandparents may have resented
even normal childhood expenses—school fees, allow-
ances, new shoes and clothes for rapidly growing
children. As a result, the second generation of O-Cs
often develops a personal preoccupation with money
and communicates a materialistic mind-set to their
own children, the third generation.

Surprisingly, materialistic thinking cuts across
economic levels. It can be seen in children of multi-
millionaires and missionaries alike. In fact, we have
observed that some of the most materialistic people
are obsessive-compulsive missionaries, pastors, and
Christian college professors. In the case of one missionary family whose income was well under the poverty level, the parents constantly communicated a
resentment about the things they didn't have and
how the family was being unjustly called on to "suffer for Jesus."

Not surprisingly, several of the children dedicated
themselves to earning large sums of money and, in
the process, became obsessive-compulsive workaholics themselves.

- *Obsessive-compulsive parents outwardly communicate that the father is the boss; however, the chil-*

dren soon learn that he is just a figurehead. The mother is actually the dominating force in the family. One obsessive-compulsive observed rather caustically, "My dad was sort of a cross between Archie Bunker and Jackie Gleason's Ralph of 'The Honeymooners.' He went around thumping his chest saying, 'I am the king of this castle.' But in reality we knew that mother was in charge."

Those are just a few of the traits we've observed in the parents of obsessive-compulsive workaholics. We have also observed that it is most common for a first-born child, regardless of his parents' personality types, to become obsessive-compulsive. Perhaps the reason is that new parents tend to expect a lot from themselves as parents and a lot from their children. As a result, they tend to be harder on their firstborn. Because they are more uptight about the process of parenting, they don't allow themselves room for error. Consequently, they cannot handle mistakes in their children because they see those mistakes as reflections on their own parental abilities. In most instances, by the time the second child arrives on the scene, the parents have mellowed in their approach to parenting. Thus, second children tend to have more problems with competing for attention than with striving for perfection. They tend to develop histrionic (or hysteric) personalities, which are emotional, excitable, overly dramatic, self-centered, manipulative, and naive. By the time the final child arrives, the parents hate to give up their controlling influence in the child's life. They tend to pamper and baby the youngest, turning that child into a passive-dependent or passive-aggressive personality who expects other people (first parents and later others) to fight all his or her battles in life.

Obviously these general principles have exceptions. However, if you are aware of the ways in which your obsessive-compulsive personality was produced, then you may be able to avoid pushing your own children too far down that same road.

7
PERFECT OR PERFECTIONIST?
A Theological Perspective

Evangelical churches today are populated with a significant number of people with obsessive-compulsive traits. These people tend to make good church workers and church leaders. Many are found in the pastorate or other forms of vocational ministry. They tend to be punctual, reliable, able to cope with responsibility, and concerned about doctrinal integrity and theological accuracy. However, from our experience in the pastorate and in counseling, we are convinced that obsessive-compulsive personality traits can often have a negative effect on a person's theological perspective.

AN EMPHASIS ON THEORY

Because of their emphasis on facts and their opposition to feelings, obsessive-compulsives tend to stress the importance of knowing theology in great detail but spend little time getting to know people—God's creation—in detail. They stress studying and understanding Scripture and theology but see little value in reading fiction or biographies, both of which contain insights into the nature of people—their needs, reactions, ambitions, and views of life. Though it is true that the apostle Paul emphasized accurate doctrine, many modern obsessive-compulsives tend to go beyond Paul to "split hairs," sometimes over questionable issues.

Paul's writings in Romans 14 and 1 Corinthians 8 demonstrate how the obsessive characteristic of black-and-white thinking creates theological difficulties. A recent survey in the largest evangelical seminary in America noted that approximately 75 percent of the students were firstborns. The overwhelming majority of those students indicated that they enrolled in the seminary because of their agreement with its doctrinal position and their concern for proper interpretation of Scripture.

This obsessiveness in theology can be both a strength and a weakness. It is important to fulfill the mandate expressed in Jude 3 to "contend for the faith," and Paul's instruction to Timothy to correctly handle the word of truth (2 Timothy 2:15). Obsessive-compulsive personality traits can certainly motivate us toward doctrinal integrity and appropriate exercise of separation from the world. However, when taken to the extreme, obsessive thinking can lead to doctrinal hair-splitting while ignoring the weightier matters of the Law. Obsessives may develop a tendency toward oppositional thinking and debate, practices for which Jesus condemned the Pharisees:

> Woe to you, teachers of the law and Pharisees, you hypocrites! You give a tenth of your spices—mint, dill and cummin. But you have neglected the more important matters of the law—justice, mercy and faithfulness. You should have practiced the latter, without neglecting the former. [Matthew 23:23]

A Sunday school teacher at an evangelical church is an excellent case in point. When he relocated from one Midwestern city to another, it took him almost a year to find a church with which he was comfortable and a pastor whose teaching he could respect. Yet, almost immediately he began tearing apart the church's constitution and doctrinal statement, pointing out what he perceived to be inaccuracies that needed modifications.

At the end of each service, he made a beeline to the pastor, eager to point out statements he had "caught" during the service or to clarify issues he felt the pastor had not sufficiently resolved in the message. Given a Sunday school class to teach, he became bogged down in such intensive detail that many of the class members left in frustration. Those people he promptly condemned as being unspiritual, disinterested in the truth, and of a lesser commitment than he. On a regular basis, he threatened to quit the church, and finally, after several sessions with the board of elders, he fulfilled his threats. Finding another church, he soon began to repeat the same obsessive cycle. Although he had many positive obsessive traits, including his concern for doctrinal accuracy, his obsessive overkill actually produced more spiritual harm than good.

Another obsessive-compulsive church member strongly encouraged his church to drop what he called "preliminary trappings" such as music. The pastor and elders refused, citing numerous scriptural exhortations to sing and examples of the proper place of music and other worship activities in the service. Then he began criticizing the *content* of the music, looking for anything he considered to be "doctrinally inaccurate." A major conflict developed between this individual and the minister of music in the church. Most of the congregation were polarized around the resulting schism.

HIDDEN PERSONAL DOUBTS

Ironically, obsessive-compulsives tend to come across as having a theological handle on every doctrinal issue, yet frequently they are privately plagued with personal doubts. In fact, they are one of the most likely groups of people to experience doubts of salvation, even after trusting Christ as Savior. In a sense, those doubts can take the form of a "theological panic attack." They are not rooted in any objective reality but seem to stem from the conditional love the obsessive received as a child from his father. Because a great deal of our thinking about our heavenly Father is formed by our earthly father, it makes sense that if our earthly father loved us conditionally and rejected us when we failed to perform, we attribute the same responses to our heavenly Father when we fail Him. Thus, when obsessive-compulsives rebel against God, disobey, fall into sin, or even when they are rationally working out their salvation, they often begin to experience doubts about their salvation.

INABILITY TO TRUST

This is also related to another trait of obsessives —difficulty in trusting. A rather interesting observation regarding the theology of obsessive-compulsives is that they tend to gravitate toward a rather strong Calvinistic position with an emphasis on the sovereignty of God.

People who have predominantly hysterical traits tend to take a more emotionally involved approach to their faith. Those who have a high degree of obsessive-compulsive traits, on the other hand, have a tendency to take an intellectual approach to faith and are more doctrinally oriented.

We are strongly committed to the sovereignty of God, but we believe in a balanced approach that also includes personal responsibility.

One of the reasons people hold to the all-encompassing sovereignty of God is to give themselves a sense of control in a seemingly uncertain world. Many people who are classified as "hypercalvinistic" have taken that position for a very interesting reason. Each would probably stress that he or she took that position because of a personal study of the Scriptures and related literature. However, in our counseling experience we have seen many of these individuals made aware that they emphasize the sovereignty of God so completely in order to develop a sense of control in an uncertain world and at times even to try to avoid personal responsibility for certain areas of misconduct. Sometimes an obsessive-compulsive struggles with the presence of evil in the world when he or she really has trouble with the evil in his or her own heart. One of the ways in which many obsessives cope with that is by adopting an extreme hypercalvinistic position—"whatever happens was meant to be."

We are convinced that obsessive-compulsives tend to make excellent theologians, gifted pastors, biblical expositors, and highly competent teachers. However, it is important for obsessives to gain insight into the relationship between the theological positions they adopt and their personality traits. Because they are such perfectionists, they have trouble accepting the fact that they are imperfect. An inability to handle their own imperfection causes them to doubt the reality of the commitment they made in trusting Christ. Then, when they do sin or even err with the best of intentions, they may feel that somehow they have lost their salvation. This occurs on a feeling level in spite of the fact that most of them profess to believe in the Christian's "eternal security."

8
AT THE END OF MY ROPE

John was a dedicated, hard-working student who graduated from college with superior marks. During seminary he was highly motivated and anticipated a successful ministry. Following seminary he entered a pastorate, where he began implementing his goals for what he called a "biblical, New Testament church." Within a year, the church was wracked by conflict. John resigned, disillusioned. Compounding his frustration were conflicts in his marriage, conflicts that could be traced largely to his perfectionistic tendencies. John was experiencing two important consequences of extreme obsessive behavior—personal burnout and marital conflict.

PERSONAL BURNOUT

Within the last decade, psychologists such as Herbert Freudenberger have popularized the term *burnout*, a term defined by Christiana Maslach as "a cluster of symptoms, including emotional and physical exhaustion, depersonalization or a tendency to withdraw from people, and decreased personal and professional performance" (*Burnout: The Cost of Caring* [Englewood, N.J.: Prentice-Hall, 1982], p. 3). In our counseling ministries, we are seeing more and more people suffering from burnout. These include not only perfectionistic homemakers, factory workers, and farmers but also hardcharging executives and people involved in such caring professions as medicine, Christian ministry, and counseling.

What are the factors that cause a large number of people with obsessive-compulsive traits to suffer burnout? Let's look at the major ones.

IDEALISM

Obsessive-compulsives tend to have a high number of idealistic expectations. Obsessive-compulsive pastors like John anticipate that people will come to hear all their sermons, integrate the messages into their experience, and noticeably grow as Christians. An obsessive-compulsive expects an enthusiastic response to new programs, a willingness to become involved in work projects, and faithful attendance at committee and activity meetings.

However, when people prove themselves to be people—indifferent to many of the Bible study programs and church services, unwilling or unable to attend the multiple church meetings and functions, and simply too tired or too indifferent to become involved in work projects—the obsessive-compulsive pastor's idealism is shattered, and that frequently leads to burnout.

BITTERNESS

Closely related to idealism and unfulfilled expectations is bitterness, the most significant factor in burnout. Bitterness, which involves prolonging anger with a vengeance motive, is the result of holding grudges. It is an even greater factor in burnout than current stresses or perfectionistic personality traits. (For a more detailed treatment of this factor, see our book *How to Beat Burnout.*)

When our idealistic expectations about marriage, work relationships, material gains, or other factors in life are not met, the natural result is for us to feel angry toward someone or something. We may be angry at our spouse for not being the "perfect marriage partner" (even though we ourselves are imperfect), angry at our supervisor or fellow workers for failing to appreciate our efforts to improve the quality of work in the workplace, or even angry with God for failing to recognize our efforts or for allowing us to suffer adversity.

Such anger is expressed in two statements by the prophet Isaiah: "Why do you say, O Jacob, and complain, O Israel, 'My way is hidden from the Lord; my cause is disregarded by my God'?" (40:27). Here Isaiah articulates on behalf of Israel the two statements commonly heard from people today who suffer from burnout:

1. "Nobody sees or appreciates the adversity I am experiencing—not even God!"

The second is similar to it, but subtly different.

2. "Life isn't fair. I'm getting a raw deal."

When our idealism is shattered, we start to feel that life isn't fair, and we naturally look around for someone or something to blame. The anger produced by blame confronts us with a choice. We must either choose immediately to forgive, as God instructs us in Ephesians 4:26, "Do not let the sun go down while you are still angry"—or by default we will choose to harbor anger and resentment, which ultimately leads to bitterness and easily infects those around us (Hebrews 12:15). Bitterness can affect marriage relationships (Colossians 3:19), as well as other relationships. As we have seen, bitterness can quickly lead to burnout.

William, a young Bible college graduate, was invited to join the staff of a rapidly growing church in the Southeast. At first he functioned well in his assistant pastor's role, although, as he shared with his senior pastor, "I consider every situation an ideal one." Within a matter of weeks, his idealism began to be shattered by the realization of the harsh facts of life— husbands lose their jobs or are just unwilling to work; wives are caught up in materialism and gossip; parents demand appropriate behavior from children without showing a willingness to relate to them or show them love; children are indifferent to parents or spiritual issues; and church people just don't seem to care.

Within a year, William was invited to serve as pastor of a small nearby church. He told his wife that he was thrilled with the opportunity to finally be able to motivate people himself. "Up until now I've felt that part of our problem has been our senior pastor. If he only had the right commitment and vision, our church would be moving by now."

When he settled into his own small church, however, William once again collided with the harsh realities of life. His new congregation met in a building that desperately needed improvements and repairs. When he pointed out the need for a renovation project in what he considered to be a tactful way, the response ranged from, "We were satisfied with this building before you came," to, "Who do you think you are, you young whippersnapper?" It wasn't long before William began preaching a series of scathing sermons designed to invoke the wrath of God on what he called "my carnal, indifferent people."

Soon things went from bad to worse. Within a year, William resigned, relocated his family a thousand miles away, and decided to have no further contact with Christians. All that occurred within two years of graduating at the top of his Bible college class, where he had been recognized as one of the graduates with the potential for a long-term ministry for Christ.

What had happened? William had clung to his idealism, which resulted in unfulfilled expectations. That led to holding grudges and anger, which resulted in burnout.

MEASURING BURNOUT

How can you tell if you are burning out?

Burnout is approaching:

- if you find yourself griping more and more and enjoying it less and less;
- if you can't stand people;
- if you want to withdraw;
- if you feel like the school bus driver who said, "I love my bus; I like my route, but I hate every single student who rides my bus";
- if you have trouble separating people from their performance, especially if no one's performance matches up to your rigorous standards;
- if you are experiencing drug or alcohol abuse;
- if you have had a major blowup—yelling at people or collapsing in tears;
- if you have felt "paralyzed" when you needed to take action.

Burnout is probably acute:

- if you have experienced a coronary or other serious physical problem;

- if you are experiencing an emotional breakdown or suicidal feelings;
- if you are involved in "acting-out" behavior—an affair, an arrest for driving while intoxicated (burnout doesn't excuse sinful behavior but may explain why it occurs);
- if you are completely overcome by exhaustion or uncontrollable anger.

Burnout has become chronic:

- if you continually find yourself withdrawing physically from your job;
- if you have trouble maintaining contact with people—even eye contact or verbal communication;
- if you quit your job without good reason;
- if you lack the emotional energy to handle the daily hassles of family life;
- if you refuse to discuss your problems or acknowledge a need for help.

BEATING BURNOUT

How can the perfectionistic obsessive-compulsive suffering from burnout deal with it? For an individual to beat burnout, we are convinced that a comprehensive approach is absolutely necessary. To be successful, the individual must take a number of steps.

First, he must deal with current causes of stress, including his frantic schedule of "burning the candle at both ends and in the middle." Many people have found it necessary to quit one of the two full-time jobs they were trying to sustain, or to take a less demanding position, even at lower pay.

Second, he must correct physical stress by taking needed steps, including proper exercise, rest, and diet.

Third, he must realistically assess his goals and schedules.

Fourth, he must pay attention to the effects of his personality type and deal with his early environment factors (those unmet, idealistic expectations left over from childhood). As Mark Twain once pointed out, "It's not what you eat that destroys you; it's what eats you."

Fifth, he must learn to give up grudges and bitterness, choosing to forgive those with whom he is bitter, even if they don't deserve forgiveness. The emotional energy used to harbor those unresolved grudges and feelings of anger can often be redirected to useful pursuits surprisingly quickly when burnout victims *choose* to make peace with their emotions by forgiving those people who have let them down, including themselves.

Ultimately, forgiving others and ourselves is possible only when we have experienced God's forgiveness by placing our faith in the Lord Jesus Christ as our Savior from sin and its consequences. He died on the cross and rose again so that we might experience God's forgiveness from all our sins. Once we come to trust in Him and experience His forgiveness, we are in a position to forgive others who have offended us. We then can appropriate God's strength to face the pressures of life.

Two passages of Scripture give us a clue as to how this is done in the context of living the Christian life. Isaiah 40:31 points out that those who "*wait* upon the Lord shall renew their strength; they shall mount up with wings as eagles; they shall run, and not be weary; and they shall walk, and not faint" (KJV, italics added). The word Isaiah uses for *wait* does not imply a passive resignation but an active anticipation that God will provide the energy and will work within circumstances. A key New Testament principle can be seen in Matthew 6:33-34, where Jesus instructs His followers to seek first His kingdom and righteousness. Once God's kingdom and His righteousness have been made a priority, everything else falls into its rightful place. Furthermore, the Savior adds that it is inappropriate to be anxious or distracted about tomorrow, for "tomorrow will worry about itself. Each day has enough trouble of its own" (v. 34). The principle is obvious. One of the keys to beating burnout is to live life one day at a time, trusting God for grace for each experience we encounter, and not dwelling on our past mistakes or on harmful actions that were initiated against us. Neither are we to focus on the future, wondering what is going to happen to us next. Rather, we are to claim God's grace for the here and now.

MARITAL CONFLICT

The second major consequence of extreme obsessive-compulsive behavior involves the marriage relationship. In Frank Minirth's research on the obsessive-compulsive personality type, a number of characteristics are isolated that weaken the marriage relationship when they are present in the extreme. Even in courtship, the obsessive-compulsive tends to be characterized by caution or restraint. In some respects, this is a positive trait, preventing premarital sexual involvement or making a commitment to the wrong person. However, some obsessives can be so perfectionistic in their courtship that they never find the "perfect" mate.

Making a marriage commitment is extremely difficult for the perfectionist since he tends to live in the future a great deal of the time, working for a tomorrow that never arrives. A marriage commitment in the here and now can be a risky venture.

Once married, O-Cs have other problems. For example, Jerry, a successful businessman with many O-C traits, demanded that his wife, Julie, be totally loyal to him. In fact, he often became infuriated with her when she gave time to the church or to other people, demanding that she "fulfill her God-given role" to meet his needs. Despite his demands on his wife, Jerry had trouble recognizing that he himself was far from totally committed to his wife. Instead, he was a workaholic who was committed to his job "110 percent." He often worked overtime and weekends, frequently forgetting to call his wife to let her know that he would not be home in time to enjoy the meal that he still expected her to prepare so carefully.

Jerry's attitude illustrates several other difficulties O-Cs encounter in their marriage relationships.

1. *They give minimal commitment but demand maximal commitment.* Obsessives seem to have a tendency to think of themselves as being more committed than they really are. They often give themselves credit for not being involved in sexual affairs, counting that restraint as true loyalty to their partners. They fail to see the disloyalty in their workaholism or in their unwillingness to share themselves, that is, to communicate their basic, inner feelings.

2. *They limit intimacy.* Obsessives have an intense fear of vulnerability or lack of control, which includes emotional vulnerability. To express feelings is to give up a measure of control and to admit weakness, something the obsessive dares not do.

3. *They need to control both themselves and those around them.* That need frequently results in power struggles within a marriage, especially if both spouses are strong O-Cs. In such cases, control can ex-

tend from such petty issues as whether the toothpaste tube is squeezed from the end or the middle to such major issues as vocation or the number of children desired.

4. *They do only (what they consider to be) their share in the marriage.* This leads to a kind of "50-50" marriage relationship, one we have seen to be less than ideal or successful. Our conviction is that a marriage can be successful only when both partners give 100 percent to the relationship. When one, or both of them, looks to do only his share, resentments and conflict will naturally build.

5. *They experience unspontaneous and routine sexual function.* Female obsessives may have difficulty with orgasms. Males may encounter difficulty with premature ejaculation, caused by anxiety or a fear of loss of control. Frequently, over a period of time, obsessives will have a tendency to ignore the physical dimension of communication in marriage, replacing sexual harmony and spontaneity and emotional and verbal communication with an increased commitment to work or to acquiring and enjoying material things.

We have seen marriages in which both partners pursued their individual interests for years. Although they lived under the same roof, they were like ships passing in the night. The husband had his work, his golf, his fishing, and his interest in football; the wife had her tennis and her social club or church activities. In some marriages the only commonalities were the children and the problems. It's no wonder that such marriages die on the vine. Since obsessive-compulsives have a great capacity to work and to exhibit commitment, it's sad that they fear commitment in interpersonal relationships and therefore fail to work on the area that God considers a high priority—marital harmony.

We encourage obsessives to give up perfectionism in marriage, to avoid bitterness, to work on sharing personal communication verbally, not just physically, and to learn to enjoy their partner as a good friend as well as a fellow heir "of the grace of life."

We have examined two consequences of O-C behavior: personal burnout and marital conflict. However, those consequences need not come to pass. In the next chapter, we will consider some ways to cure excessive obsessive-compulsive behavior.

9
REACHING BALANCE
OR BURNOUT?

A pastor/counselor was invited to address the annual meeting of a large mental health facility in northern Illinois. The subject was the relationship between stress and obsessive behavior. As the speaker walked into the facility where the meeting was being held, he was met by the mental health administrator who said, "Do I need to hear what you have to say! I hope you have some practical suggestions for getting a handle on my own stress and obsessiveness."

That same desire has been voiced to us by individuals from all walks of life. Many obsessives suffer periodic obsessive-compulsive disorders, receive counseling, and are aware of their unbalanced obsessive behavior. But they realize that simply understanding it, or even tracing it to its early childhood origin, doesn't do anything to reverse it.

Put another way, most perfectionists find that insight into the nature of their difficulties is not sufficient to effect change. We have found a total revamping of *attitudes* to be necessary, including (1) gaining insight into thought processes, (2) developing interpersonal relational skills, and (3) acquiring the motivation to change.

Some counselors say the way to overcome extreme obsessive-compulsive behavior is to remove all structure from counseling. Instead of giving specific direction, the counselor should simply provide support and encouragement.

The problem with that approach is that O-Cs have difficulty expressing their feelings, and they tend to be more comfortable with a high degree of structure. Often a counselor will simply try to get an obsessive-compulsive to remove all structure and organization from his or her life; however, the real issue is not structure or lack of it but an inability to get in touch with personal feelings. Removing all structure from one's life can actually hinder the process of balancing obsessive behavior.

STEPS TO OVERCOME O-C BEHAVIOR

We suggest the following practical steps, based on a survey of effective programs and on our own experience in dealing with obsessive behavior.

MAKE AN ADVANTAGE/DISADVANTAGE LIST

The first step is to make a list of the advantages and disadvantages of perfectionism. Then weigh the benefits against the costs. In this way obsessives can call into play familiar and often-used skills to help assess their perfectionism.

This process will hopefully bring about an awareness, perhaps for the first time, that perfectionism or obsessive-compulsive behaviors do not always produce positive results. This awareness, in turn, can provide a motivation to give up the imbalances in obsessiveness.

One obsessive, Julie, came up with the following interesting lists.

Advantages:

1. Obsessive behavior helps me produce quality work.

2. It also helps me produce a greater quantity of work.

Disadvantages:

1. I'm often so uptight I sometimes have trouble producing quality work.

2. My rigidity and perfectionism tend to stifle my creativity and my willingness to try novel approaches.

3. I constantly find myself criticizing myself and others. This takes all the fun out of relationships and the rest of my life.

4. I have trouble walking away from my responsibility. In fact, I sometimes have trouble relaxing.

Her conclusion: To be an imbalanced perfectionist is counterproductive.

DISCOVER NEW WAYS TO HANDLE STRESS

The second step is to discover less obsessive ways to handle the stress factors in your life. Again, a list or form of written evaluation can be helpful. Write down various stress factors, both major and minor, and then decide which ones you can influence and which ones you have no control over. Many obsessives have found help from the prayer of St. Francis of Assisi: "God grant me the serenity to accept those things that cannot be changed, the courage to change those which can, and the wisdom to know the difference."

Three keys can help us manage those stress factors that often add to the misery of imbalanced obsessive behavior.

First, learn to be assertive. Frequently, an O-Cs problem is either the inability to say no or the inability to say no graciously. Obsessives tend to adopt extreme "either-or" thinking; therefore, they are either passive, allowing others to run them over, or they become aggressive after just "taking it" for a long time and lash out at the people and circumstances producing the stress. A balanced approach to handling stress involves some assertiveness.

Assertiveness is the ability to stand up for one's rights, to express one's true feelings when appropriate—without fear of reprisal, to be able to say no to unreasonable demands, and to request the things we need and deserve.

Foundational to appropriate assertiveness is the basic underlying message "I count, and you count." If we refuse to be assertive, we are either saying, "I count, and you don't count" (which is aggressiveness), or, "You count, but I don't count" (which is nonassertiveness or passivity). The following list of suggested assertive statements can help obsessive-compulsives and others who need to become more balanced in this area.

"No, I won't do that."
"That makes me angry."
"I disagree with you."
"This really bothers me."
"Please stop doing that."
"Will you help me?"
"I really like that about you."

"I think you're not being fair."
"I need something from you."
"Thank you, but I don't care to."
"It hurts my feelings when you say things like that."
"There are some things I think we need to get straightened out."

Second, learn proper time management. Although many obsessives tend to overdo time management, they sometimes ignore good time management principles, including preparing for future events. Because they are so successful at being achievement-oriented, they frequently leave unfinished tasks for the last minute, assuming they have the ability to accomplish in minutes what takes other people hours and days. Type A O-Cs often see themselves as almost superhuman. Unfortunately, unforeseen snags are likely to trip them up. We have discovered through personal experience the wisdom of the old proverb "An ounce of prevention is worth a pound of cure."

Third, delegate to others when possible. One of the obsessive's favorite sayings is, "Thanks, but I'd rather do it myself." That's not usually an appropriate assertive response (although it can be under certain circumstances). Usually it indicates an unwillingness to relinquish control.

CORRECT FAULTY THINKING

Balancing obsessive behavior also involves correcting the flaws in our thinking. According to Chris Thurman in *The Lies We Believe*, a good place to start is to notice carefully our "self-talk," comparing it with inaccurate things or lies we tell ourselves ([Nashville: Thomas Nelson, 1989], pp. 35-57).

We sometimes suggest that obsessives keep a daily written record of self-critical thoughts and statements or that they ask a spouse or close friend to hold them accountable for their self-talk. Sometimes self-talk habits become automatic thoughts. As obsessives write them down, they are able to pinpoint inaccuracies and develop more objective and appropriate ways to talk to themselves.

Four of the more common unhealthy messages we give ourselves are:
"I must be perfect."
"I should please others."
"I must try harder."
"Life must be fair."

For example, Jeanne, a graduate student, faced a Monday deadline on a paper, in addition to an exam. However, family and work responsibilities caused her to have an extremely busy weekend with very little time for preparation. On Monday Jeanne hit the panic button.

Under those circumstances, hitting the panic button was not necessarily a bad thing to do. However, undergirding Jeanne's thinking was the feeling, *I've failed miserably. I didn't get my studying done this weekend. I allowed my schedule to get out of control. I'm a failure as a person. I'm a failure as a student. I will fail in the future.*

Furthermore, while she typed her paper Jeanne made several mistakes. Again, in her personal self-assessment, this was an unpardonable sin. Her thoughts: *The professor will certainly notice all these errors. He will think the paper is poorly thought out. He'll consider me an irresponsible student. He'll be sure I don't really care about doing well. I'll probably wind up with an F, or a D at best.*

Although we might be quick to recognize the "all or nothing" inaccuracy in Jeanne's thinking (she had some of the highest marks in the class), we ourselves have a tendency to fall into the same trap of irrational thinking.

Albert Ellis in his book *A New Guide to Rational Living* (Wilshire, 1975, p. 82), has identified a number of common irrational beliefs that are found frequently among obsessive-compulsive Christians. Here are some of those beliefs.

I must be perfect in order to feel worthwhile. However, the Scriptures tell us, "All have sinned and fall short of the glory of God" (Romans 3:23).

I must have everyone's love and/or approval. Again, the truth from Scripture is that no one will feel total approval at any time. Many people certainly didn't approve of Jesus Christ. He Himself said, "No servant is greater than his master. If they persecuted me, they will persecute you also" (John 15:20).

It is horrible or catastrophic when things don't go the way I want them to. A classic refutation of this is the prayer of Christ in the Garden of Gethsemane, "Father, if you are willing, take this cup from me; yet not my will, but yours be done" (Luke 22:42; cf. Mark 14:36; Matthew 26:39).

It is easier to avoid problems than to face them. Again, in the Garden of Gethsemane, Jesus told His disciples, "Arise, let us be going," and told them with full knowledge of His impending crucifixion.

Human unhappiness is caused externally. This idea is in clear contradiction to Paul's assertion in Philippians 4:11, "I have learned, in *whatsoever state I am*, therewith to be content" (KJV, italics added).

Life should be fair. One of the most obvious victims of injustice in human history was Job, yet he was able to assert, "He knows the way that I take; when he has tested me, I will come forth as gold" (Job 23:10).

Life should be easy. From his personal experience Paul wrote to the Philippians, "It has been granted to you on behalf of Christ not only to believe on him, but also to suffer for him" (Philippians 1:29). Also, 2 Timothy 3:12 says, "In fact, everyone who wants to live a godly life in Christ Jesus will be persecuted."

Correcting the flaws in our thinking involves an awareness, even though it may be painful, of the defense mechanisms we use to deceive ourselves. As we discussed earlier, some common defense mechanisms we use are: *intellectualization*, to avoid facing our emotions; *magical thinking*, to fool ourselves into trying to do more than we can accomplish; *reaction formation*, to develop acceptable attitudes and behavior to hide our lustful, greedy, or power-hungry thoughts from ourselves and from others; *undoing*, to compensate for the unacknowledged anger we feel toward others; *isolation*, to separate sinful areas of our lives from the reality we perceive about ourselves. It is imperative that we come to grips with these flaws in our thinking, confess them as sin (1 John 1:9), and allow God to deal with them.

Facing distorted thinking is difficult for practicing obsessives. The following checklist by Aaron Beck can help an obsessive recognize the distorted way he looks at reality:

Magnification—making a mountain out of a molehill

Personalization—relating everything that happens to yourself

Polarization—seeing everything in black or white, including nonabsolutes

Overgeneralization—making blanket judgments or predictions on the basis of a single incident

Selective abstraction—focusing on a single detail out of context

Emotional reasoning—treating facts as feelings

One of the most important keys to overcoming imbalanced obsessive *behavior* is to correct imbalanced obsessive *thinking*. As Jesus Christ so clearly pointed out, "As [a man] thinketh in his heart, so is he" (Proverbs 23:7, KJV). Balanced thinking will lead to balanced living.

IMPROVE YOUR ABILITY TO RELATE TO OTHERS

Unbalanced obsessives tend to take a "lone ranger" approach to life. Yet, even the Lone Ranger found it important to depend upon his faithful sidekick, Tonto, when facing adversity.

We see two aspects of this "people factor."

First, develop a network of significant people for support. Proverbs 18:24 says "there is a friend who sticks closer than a brother." Clearly developing friendships is an active, not a passive, matter. Because imbalanced obsessives tend to be more task-oriented than people-oriented, this is an area to which they need to devote themselves. Look for people with whom you are like-minded, people with whom you share values, interests, and goals. Work at accepting them unconditionally, that is, "giving them some slack," when they don't live up to your expectations. Treat them with the time-worn Golden Rule, as you would like them to treat you—*not* in the way you feel they have actually treated you. Loyalty and love, extended even in times of adversity, are the soil in which friendships grow (cf. Proverbs 17:17). And Proverbs 27 is replete with the benefits of having good friends in our lives (Proverbs 27:6, 9, 10, 17).

One of us has adopted a personal goal of developing one good friendship every two to three years. Frank Minirth says, "I find that I cannot develop really close friendships any more quickly than this. Developing good friends is hard work. But I've also discovered that having good friends with whom I can share my feelings is essential to my own mental and spiritual well-being."

Sometimes it can be helpful for O-Cs to develop or become part of support groups designed for the purpose of sharing friendships. One of us has been involved for some years with a group of obsessive-compulsives known as OCWA—the "Obsessive-Compulsive Workaholics Anonymous" group. Started informally, it has provided both mutual support and a number of mental health-producing laughs as well. Perhaps OCWA chapters will now spring up in other places around the country.

Second, learn to communicate feelings. For the obsessive, communicating facts is easier than expressing emotions. "I feel" messages are almost like a foreign language to many O-Cs. We suggest that obsessives develop a specific time to share feelings with their spouse and have an agreement with a few good friends, in the context of unconditional love, to feel free to express feelings whenever they need to do so.

Scripture commands that we get together to encourage one another. Hebrews 10:25, the passage often used by obsessive pastors and church leaders to produce guilt over laxity in church attendance, is in reality an exhortation to all believers to practice mutual encouragement and exhortation or, in more simple terms, to learn to communicate with other Christians.

GET TO KNOW AND ACCEPT YOURSELF

Get to know yourself, accept yourself, and become all God wants you to be in Christ. Thousands of Christians have memorized Romans 12:1-2, but few can quote verse 3. It is one of the most important verses in Scripture in terms of Christian living: "For by the grace given to me I say to every one of you: Do not think of yourself more highly than you ought, but rather think of yourself with sober judgment, in accordance with the measure of faith God has given you."

The point is that we need to come to a realistic appraisal of our personality, abilities, and unique God-given design. The clearest and most obvious danger is to think of ourselves more highly than we should, and Paul warns against that. But many of us react to the other extreme and spend a lot of time putting ourselves down. The authors have developed a motto to help implement Romans 12:3 in our personal lives. It is: *Strengthen your strengths while working on your weaknesses.*

Here is a practical suggestion: take a sizable chunk of time, sit down, reflect on yourself, and make a list of your strengths and abilities. Perhaps you are highly organized. Maybe you are a self-starter. Perhaps you have an ability to grasp intellectual material. You may be an excellent communicator. Write down those strengths. Then begin listing ways you can improve them.

When U.S. Congressman Bill Bradley was in high school, he worked one summer on Capitol Hill. Each evening he stopped by a high school gym. He picked out six or eight spots on the court from which to shoot baskets, and he wouldn't leave until he had made fifty shots from each. Bradley became an excellent shot because his hard work and patience paid off. He ultimately became an All-American at Princeton University and a highly successful professional basketball player for the New York Knicks before he ran for Congress.

Although spending time in strengthening your strengths is a worthy investment, make sure you don't overdo this to the detriment of other important areas of life. To do so will only weaken the base of your strengths.

Rachel grew up in a home in which relationships were primarily characterized by conditional love. Love was shown only when a family member did something that especially pleased another family member. Rachel's father loved her mother conditionally, and both parents practiced conditional love toward the children.

Because Rachel was the oldest and her parents had particularly high expectations for her, she was most affected by their conditional love. Thus taught, she found herself developing conditional love toward other people around her.

After trusting Christ as her Savior in high school, Rachel came into contact with Christians who had strong convictions about how to live the Christian life but who also practiced conditional love. Thus, conditional love was reinforced in her life even after she became a Christian.

Not until she moved away from home and met Christians at college and in a collegiate church that reached out to her with unconditional love did she begin to develop the ability to love and accept others, despite their failures and weaknesses. Through counseling, she was directed to use her obsessive-compulsive traits to work at practicing unconditional love instead of accepting others only on the basis of her own high standards of performance. It was a struggle; yet it ultimately paid off. Eventually, Rachel became known in her church family, among a wide circle of friends at college, and later at work as a person who could be counted on for unconditional love and encouragement.

One of the obsessive-compulsive's greatest strengths is a willingness to work. We suggest that obsessives pay attention not only to strengthening strengths, but also to working hard on their weaknesses—even harder than they do on their strengths, that is, on handling emotions, accepting and loving people unconditionally, or organizing areas of their lives that tend to escape order altogether. Whatever the weakness, the obsessive must work on it diligently.

LEARN TO LIVE IN THE PRESENT

Learn to live life in the present—one day at a time. Because obsessives tend to be people of extremes, they frequently find themselves living in the past, plagued with guilt. Sometimes it is *true guilt* over unconfessed sin, which their defense mechanisms have fooled them into sinfully denying. But sometimes it is *false guilt* over sins they have confessed and know God has forgiven, but for which they have failed to forgive themselves. Because Christ has forgiven us for every sin we have committed, we can confess them, then forget about them—refuse to dwell on them (Philippians 3:14).

For other obsessives a major problem involves their living in the future. They are anxious about what tomorrow may bring, and that intense anxiety distracts them. In fact, distraction is the basic concept behind the Greek word used for anxiety in the New Testament. Such distraction keeps them from enjoying life. Remember that Jesus said, "I have come that they may have life, and have it to the full" (John 10:10).

Because Christ holds the future securely in His hands, we can stop being anxious about tomorrow, for tomorrow will take care of itself (Matthew 6:34). The realistic obsessive-compulsive is an individual who learns to live one day at a time, without being haunted by the past or being overly concerned about the future. In other words, if life gives you a hot fudge sundae, eat it without feeling guilty but at the same time without gluttony.

An obsessive can become a truly balanced, highly productive individual—one who serves God and relates effectively both with God and other people. He can do so by establishing daily priorities consistent with his life goals, by learning to distinguish the important from the urgent, by obeying Jesus' instruction to wholeheartedly love God and unconditionally love people (Mark 12:30-31).

10
HUMAN ABILITY AND DIVINE ENABLEMENT

Occasionally an individual walks across the pages of history and leaves footprints that later generations interpret to be larger than life. Such an individual was Moses. It didn't really take the brush of Hollywood cinematographers to paint this man in grand and glowing terms. In fact, a first-century church leader named Stephen, in the sermon that cost him his life, described Moses as an incredibly gifted individual (Acts 7:20-22). Apparently, Stephen was familiar with the biblical evidence, the traditions, and the historical information passed down about Moses, the man who played such a critical role in his nation's history.

Stephen described Moses as physically beautiful. In fact, according to the historian Josephus, Moses was a man of such exceptional strength and beauty that the Egyptians would crowd around just to get a look at him.

Yet Moses' physical assets did not overshadow his intellectual accomplishments, which Stephen describes in Acts 7:22. From his infancy to the time he became a young man, Moses received an excellent education in the royal palace of Egypt. The Egypt of Moses' day was the most progressive and productive country in the world. Moses was exposed to the kind of training that led to the building of the pyramids—mathematics, engineering, art, and architecture. As the chosen heir to the king, he received a tailored course of study designed to equip him for political leadership and warfare.

This leads to a third key quality that Stephen describes: Moses' leadership abilities. In the simple phrase "powerful in speech and action," Stephen captures the essence of what made Moses such a great leader of men. Other incidents from Josephus's records illustrate Moses' leadership ability. When the Ethiopians attacked Egypt, Egypt was on the verge of defeat. Moses was appointed general in charge of the army, and under his leadership the tide turned and the Ethiopians were driven back. Certainly, if any individual had the ability to serve and please God on his own, Moses was that man.

Yet one incident in Moses' life demonstrates the difference between human ability and divine enablement. It is recorded in Exodus 3 and took place not in the palaces of Egypt but on the backside of a desert, in the arid land near Mount Sinai. At that time Moses was eighty. To understand this occurrence we must examine another incident that happened forty years earlier, when Moses was, humanly speaking, in the prime of his life. That event is recorded in Exodus 2:11-15:

> One day, after Moses had grown up, he went out to where his own people were and watched them at their hard labor. He saw an Egyptian beating a Hebrew, one of his own people. Glancing this way and that and seeing no one, he killed the Egyptian and hid him in the sand. The next day he went out and saw two Hebrews fighting. He asked the one in the wrong, "Why are you hitting your fellow Hebrew?"
> The man said, "Who made you ruler and judge over us? Are you thinking of killing me as you killed

the Egyptian?" Then Moses was afraid and thought,
"What I did must have become known."

When Pharaoh heard of this, he tried to kill Moses, but Moses fled from Pharaoh and went to live in
Midian, where he sat down by a well.

Moses was a gifted man, keenly aware of his mission in life. He was trained with the wisdom of the
Egyptians and possessed strong leadership skills. Furthermore, he decided to become involved with the servant race from which he came, Israel. He took the life
of a man who was persecuting one of his Hebrew kins-
men, perhaps expecting that action to prompt support
and ultimately lead to Israel's liberation. After all, according to Hebrews 11:26, "he regarded disgrace for
the sake of Christ as of greater value than the trea-
sures of Egypt."

We might say that Moses burned brightly for a day;
but because he depended on his own enablement "in
the flesh," or "in his own strength," he became as
burned out as a heap of ashes.

We're struck with a remarkable contrast of what
happened when Moses returned to Egypt at twice the
age he was when he had left and at a time when most
people would already have found an opportunity to re-
tire. Moses was able not only to successfully challenge
Pharaoh but also to lead the Israelites out of Egypt, tolerate their complaints and rebellion, provide them
with the written material of the Law as revealed by Je-
hovah God, and shepherd them over a tortuous route
for forty years of desert wandering.

THE BURNING BUSH

How could Moses accomplish all of that? The answer seems to lie in the incident of the burning bush.
Undoubtedly Moses had seen burning bushes before,

yet there was a remarkable difference in this bush, because the fire did not consume it. The flame was the presence of the preincarnate Christ, which turned that desert shrub into a remarkable tool of God's personal revelation to Moses.

Through the bush Moses learned of God's holiness and uniqueness, and he learned that God was special, quite different from the gods of Egypt. Through the bush Moses verbally heard of the faithfulness of the God of Abraham, Isaac, and Jacob. At this point Moses began to adjust to God's compassion and purpose to deliver Israel from Egypt and to bring His people into the Promised Land. It was also through the burning bush that God clarified the role Moses was to play: "I am sending you to Pharaoh to bring my people the Israelites out of Egypt" (Exodus 3:10).

THE PRESENCE OF GOD

What made the difference in Moses' life? How did he endure at the age of eighty what he failed to endure at forty? Hebrews 11:27 states, "He persevered because he saw him who is invisible." The major difference that enabled Moses to avoid burning out while living an extremely active and significant life is that *he lived each day with the reality of the presence of God.*

A number of years ago a Bible college student was struck by the number of books written on the subject of the spiritual life. Many people had written seemingly profound books, giving formulas and equations that would guarantee spirituality. Yet it was easy to see that writing a book on the subject did not guarantee continued spirituality. Many who had written such books ultimately experienced significant spiritual failure.

On the other hand, many who had never written or taught on the subject obviously experienced a measure of spiritual endurance that could only be called successful. After talking with such people from all walks of life—pastors and missionaries, mechanics, housewives, factory workers, businessmen, architects, engineers, and students—the common denominator became evident to the Bible college student. Those who lived each day with the *reality of the presence of God* in their lives endured. Those who lost sight of the reality of God's presence were those who became "practicing atheists."

The Greek word for "endure," *ekarterēsē,* used by the author of Hebrews, is an unusual verb appearing only in Hebrews 11:27 in the New Testament.[1] The word is used in Greek literature (Sophocles and Josephus) and means "to be strong, steadfast, to hold out." According to one respected eminent Greek *scholar, ekarterēsē* comes from a term that means to be strong.[2] Although the term is not used elsewhere in the New Testament, its two uses in the Septuagint (the Greek version of the Old Testament) are illuminating. The first use is somewhat negative and is found in Job 2:9. Job's wife bitterly said to the patriarch, "Are you still holding on to your integrity? Curse God and die!" Many individuals today who face the adversities of a Job or a Moses opt to become bitter and lose sight of the presence of God. Job, however, continued to endure. In fact, he considered his wife's suggestion to be foolish. In response, he offered the perspective that en-

1. William F. Arndt and F. Wilbur Gingrich, *A Greek English Lexicon of the Greek New Testament and Other Early Christian Literature* (Chicago: U. of Chicago, 1957), p. 406.
2. James H. Moulton and George Milligan, *The Vocabulary of the Greek New Testament* (Grand Rapids: Eerdmans, 1930), p. 322.

abled him to endure. "Shall we accept good from God, and not trouble?" (v. 10). As with Moses or Job, endurance involves an ability to put things into perspective and to see the hand of God at work in our lives on days of cloudiness, rain, and even storm as well as on days of sunshine and blessing.

A second use of *endure* in the Old Testament is suggested in Isaiah 42:14. Here Yahweh is speaking to Israel, declaring His coming intervention in the affairs of His people. He says, "For a long time I have kept silent, I have been quiet and held myself back. But now, like a woman in childbirth, I cry out, I gasp and pant. I will lay waste the mountains and hills and dry up all their vegetation." We can see that endurance is a matter of personal choice. Just as God chose when to withhold His wrath and when to exercise it, so we can choose when we will persevere and when we will give up. Moses, when faced with such a choice, chose to endure.

The essence of Moses' choice to persevere involved a commitment of faith, because Moses saw Him who was invisible. In fact, the statement of Hebrews 11:27*b*, "He persevered because he saw him who is invisible," describes the essence of what faith is all about. It is acting not on the basis of what we perceive with our five senses, but on what we know to be true from God's revelation. It is saying, "God is with me, therefore, I will not give up."

That was the perspective that allowed Moses to persevere through the exhausting years of tramping through the wilderness while listening to the complaints of his followers and suffering incredible hardship. Tugging at the back of his mind certainly were the memories of his luxurious life in Egypt. But Moses maintained the perspective that ultimately spurred him to write Psalm 90:12, "Teach us to number our days aright, that we may gain a heart of wisdom." That verse was a reflection of his commitment not to give up, even after he knew that his personal failure would prevent his entering the Promised Land.

Because of his commitment to faith in God, Moses never quit. His strength came not from his abilities, intellect, or even leadership skills, but from practicing the presence of the Lord God. That was the divine difference. Like the bush indwelt by the presence of the preincarnate Christ, Moses never used up his resources.

GOD'S RESOURCES

Some may say, "But we don't have the opportunity Moses had to speak with the Lord face to face." And Exodus 33:11 and Numbers 12:7-8 do indicate that there were times in Moses' life when he was permitted that privilege. Yet the average believer today has far more in the way of God's resources than Moses had.

THE WORD OF GOD

We have the completed written revelation of God's perspective—everything we need and all things that pertain to life and godliness (2 Peter 1:3). The Word of God gives us clear and objective guidance (2 Timothy 3:16-17). It tells us what to believe (doctrine), and when we're wrong (reproof); it gets us "back on track" (correction); and it gives us positive principles that enable us to "stay on track" in our relationship with God and others (instruction in right living).

THE HOLY SPIRIT

We also have the resource of God the Holy Spirit living within us (Romans 8:9), which was not true for Old Testament saints. He is the ultimate Counselor, the one Jesus described in John 16 as the comforter, the *paraclete* ("called along side to help"). He is the One who provides our enablement, as we walk in His power, to keep us from fulfilling the evil desires of our old nature (Galatians 5:16). Are you sensitive daily to His presence? When you are involved in work situations, do you realize that God sees the ins and outs? When you're with other people socially, do you recognize that God knows if you're harboring feelings of envy, greed, or lust? Do you realize that God knows the very thoughts and intents of your innermost being?

PRAYER

Furthermore, we have a direct and instant access line for communication with God through prayer. We may be distressed over the past or anxious over the future, yet we are instructed: "In everything, by prayer [general contact with God] and petition [specific voicing of needs], with thanksgiving [acknowledging appreciation in advance for what God will do] present your requests to God" (Philippians 4:6). When we utilize this incredible resource, the apostle Paul promises not only peace of mind (v. 7) but the presence of God in our lives (v. 9), personal enablement for trying circumstances (v. 13), and provision for every genuine need (v. 19).

Do you utilize the communication line of prayer? As you face difficult circumstances and confront temptation, do you call on God? His part is to provide the resources. Our part is to exercise responsibility, making choices that will implement those inner resources.

OUR RESPONSIBILITY

Many of us know about God's resources—the Word of God, the Spirit of God, and prayer—but we still fail to endure because we do not claim and use those resources by faith. Our responsibility, quite simply, is to make the right choices. When confronted with overwhelming circumstances, difficult challenges, or impossible tasks, we must choose. The essence of God's method of dealing with mankind throughout history is that He gives individuals opportunities to choose to obey Him and to trust Him. It is our responsibility.

The essence of our responsibility to choose can be seen in the initial failure of mankind. In Genesis 2 man was given two responsibilities in his perfect environment. The positive one was to care for his surroundings (v. 15). The negative one was to abstain from eating fruit from the tree of the knowledge of good and evil (vv. 16-17). One chapter later, man was confronted with a choice. Satan, disguised as a serpent, presented an alternative to God's instruction. Like a large-mouth bass swallowing a brass hook hidden by a plastic worm, Adam and Eve bit. The results, according to Romans 5:12, were devastating.

Like Adam and Eve, we are affected by our choices. We are tempted to quit, or to keep going when we ought to quit, in order to prove our own significance. This may lead to such sinful behavior as the lust of the flesh (sexual or other physical temptation), the lust of the eyes (material temptations), or the pride of life (power struggles). We forget that God provides the resources that enable us to make the right choices. But we must utilize those resources. Often we fail to choose appropriately because we don't trust God or obey Him. Then, like Adam, we blame others—perhaps spouse, friends, environment, or even God. Or like Eve we may claim, "The devil made me do it." Genesis 3:13*b* says, "The woman said, 'The serpent deceived me, and I ate.' " Or we may use the excuse that we didn't really understand what was happening when we made the choices.

Regardless of what excuse we use, God makes clear that we are responsible for our choices.

We can implement God's resources by meditating on and memorizing Scripture, by praying, by walking in the Spirit, by investing daily time in devotions, by developing accountability to others in the Body of Christ, and by depending on "Him who is invisible," thereby gaining strength from a day-to-day relationship with Him. The bottom line is that we are responsible for our choices. However, it is important for us to understand that although our choices are our responsibility, on our own we are *not* able.

THE CONCEPT OF WEAKNESS

It is fascinating to study the concepts of weakness and strength in Scripture. The Old Testament has a half dozen words for "weak." The most common is the term *rafeh*, which means to be feeble physically, intellectually, or morally. It is interesting that a strong individual such as David occasionally described himself as weak (2 Samuel 3:39; Psalms 6:2, 109:24).

In the New Testament the primary word translated "weak," used in several forms, is *asthenōs*. It carries the idea of stumbling or being without strength. It can indicate physical weakness or material poverty (Acts 20:35), religious or moral weakness (Romans 14:1), or physical sickness (James 5:14, 16).

One of the best ways to gain insight into the New Testament concept of weakness is to examine Paul's use of the term in his two letters to the church at Corinth. Paul experienced controversy at Corinth, partially because the Corinthians viewed Paul as being weak. Paul even admitted that some described him as appearing weak in bodily presence (2 Corinthians 10:10). Yet he explained that the weakness of God is stronger than men's strength (1 Corinthians 1:25). God has chosen to use weak things, including weak individuals (1 Corinthians 1:27).

Furthermore, God can perfect or complete strength in weakness (2 Corinthians 12:9). This is precisely what Paul experienced as he relied upon God. It is for that reason that he was able to write those inspiring words in 2 Corinthians 4:16, "Therefore we do not lose heart. Though outwardly we are wasting away, yet inwardly we are being renewed day by day." Certainly the Corinthians were a difficult group to minister to. But Paul's ministry to the church there demonstrated the same reality as did Moses' ministry to Israel. Paul, like Moses, never quit. He ran the race, he finished the course, he kept the faith (2 Timothy 4).

TEMPTATION

Many people strive to be strong, capable, and successful. Often Christians get caught up in this mindset, but it's an impossible trap. The temptations of life are real. Many succumb to sexual temptations in the lust of the flesh. In fact, the warning of 1 Corinthians 10:12 has never been more relevant than in this day in which even well-known political and religious leaders are trapped in moral sin: "So, if you think you are standing firm, be careful that you don't fall!"

Several principles, found in Paul's words to the church at Corinth (1 Corinthians 10:13), enable us to overcome temptation. First, temptation is common to all of us. No one is immune. There is no vaccine that will prevent our succumbing to it. Psychological studies have indicated that individuals with predominantly hysteric or histrionic (openly emotional and attention-seeking) traits may be more susceptible to sexual temptation. Obsessive-compulsives (habitually hard workers) may be more susceptible to materialism, and those with paranoid or fearful traits may be more susceptible to power struggles. Yet, no matter what your personality type, you can be tempted in various ways, and you might fall.

Second, God is faithful. We cannot be counted upon except when we rely upon God. Only when we endure by faith, as did Moses and Paul, can we receive the promised resources of a faithful God, who will never let us down. In fact, Paul went on to explain that God will not permit us to be tempted beyond what we are able. Keep in mind that those words were written to believers who lived in a society as permeated with sexual temptation as ours is. Opportunities for sexual misconduct, homosexual and heterosexual, abounded in Corinth. Yet Paul promises that God will, with the temptation, make a way of escape that we may be able to bear it.

SEXUAL TEMPTATION

Recently, a young man, John, came to see one of our counselors. John was miserable. While walking in downtown Dallas en route to a business appointment he noticed a lady stepping out of a department store into a wind-blown street. The wind lifted her skirt above her head. The man immediately averted his eyes, but soon became absolutely miserable, plagued with feelings of guilt.

The counselor, on the basis of James 1 and 1 Corinthians 10:13 asked, "What did you do at that moment? Did you continue to look or did you turn away?"

The young man replied, "I immediately turned away."

"Did you continue to think about the woman?"

"No, once or twice the picture of her came into my mind. When it did, I asked God to help me think about something else, and I quoted Scripture to myself."

"Well, John," the counselor replied, "I have good news for you. On the basis of James 1 it seems that you handled this matter wisely."

For temptation to conceive (become sin), two ingredients are necessary, just as two ingredients are necessary for the conception of a human baby. Essential are the contributions of both the father and mother—the egg and the sperm. Similarly, James uses the idea of conception, consisting of two parts, to show us how temptation works. We have the external event, which provides the source of temptation—perhaps a television program, a picture in a magazine, or the sight of an actual person. We also have the internal response, which, according to James, originates "out of our own lusts." We choose either to dismiss the temptation or to give in to it. Frequently and tragically, we do the latter.

A classic example of this struggle is the account of David and Bathsheba. Although David could have come down from the housetop when he first saw Bathsheba bathing in her courtyard below, he continued to linger, looking and lusting after her. He ultimately acted on those sinful desires.

As we face similar kinds of temptations, we need to remind ourselves that God not only provides us with a way to escape but He also enables us to endure, to bear the temptation.

MATERIAL TEMPTATION

God likewise makes provision for overcoming temptation in the material realm. Paul, in writing to Timothy, explains that there are those who are particularly susceptible to the love of money, which is "a root of all kinds of evil" (1 Timothy 6:10). In our day, even in the Christian community, the attainment of materialistic success is a supposed evidence of godliness. Yet Paul reminds us to withdraw from those who suppose that gain is godliness. Would Paul have been comfortable with those who preach a "prosperity gospel" today? Even casual examination of Paul's warning to Timothy (1 Timothy 6) shows us where the apostle would stand on such an issue. Paul's equation for true success is, "But godliness with contentment is great gain" (v. 6). We are to be content with the provision of our basic needs (v. 8).

However, it is important to distinguish between those "who want to *get* rich" (1 Timothy 6:9, emphasis added), and those "who *are* rich" (v. 17, emphasis added). In the case of the latter, Paul gives instructions for avoiding temptations. Those who are blessed with a great deal of God's resources are not to be high-minded. In the Dallas area we often encounter people, even Christians, who hold to the fairly widespread mentality that if you live in north Dallas or certain suburbs, drive the latest model foreign sedan, carry a certain kind of credit card, and purchase your clothes at a ritzy department store, you are superior to those who live in other parts of the city, drive anything with four wheels, and shop at less prestigious stores.

Paul warns us not to trust in uncertain riches. We may be tempted to place confidence in material resources rather than in God. Many individuals in Texas believed that the booms in oil and real estate, which produced a show of wealth in the city of Dallas second to none, would keep growing forever. When the price of oil crashed and the economy in oil-based Houston collapsed, many Dallasites said, "It can never happen here. Our economy is more diversified." And for a couple of years it didn't happen in Dallas. But eventually the people of Dallas began to realize that their economy was indirectly tied to oil, which meant that though it took longer for the Dallas business climate to be affected, it was eventually affected. Several years after oil collapsed, when Houston was beginning to climb out of its financial depression, many Dallas citizens began declaring bankruptcy. Thousands of construction projects remained unfinished or sat idle. The economic slide shattered fortunes and lives, even in "diversified" Dallas.

The positive side of Paul's warning to Timothy concerning material things would have been good advice for Dallas, too. "Put your hope in God, who richly provides us with everything for our enjoyment" (1 Timothy 6:17). God is not opposed to our enjoying good things. It's not a sin to drive a nice car or live in a comfortable home or wear new clothing. Neither is it a sin to drive a vehicle with more than one hundred thousand miles or to purchase clothing from a "nearly new shop." In fact, Paul goes on to say that those who have material things are to do good, to be rich in good works and to be ready and eager to share and give, thus laying up treasure in heaven rather than on earth.

POWER-STRUGGLE TEMPTATION

The third area of temptation—the desire to have the preeminence (1 John 2)—may be even more subtle than the temptations we encounter in the sexual or the material realms. A classic example of a man who succumbed to such temptation is Diotrephes, whom the apostle John described in 3 John 9 as "[loving] to be *first.*" That word is used in only one other passage in the New Testament, Colossians 1:18, where it describes Jesus Christ, who is, of course, the only individual who deserves to have the preeminence and who has it in all things. The truth is that there is an element of Diotrephes in each of us. We, too, can be fond of the preeminence, whether it comes from recognition on the job, the ability to influence others, or having our personal kingdoms in the local church.

Unfortunately, many church boards and committees have been infiltrated with descendants of Diotrephes, individuals who are fond of being personally recognized and who rule their little fiefdoms. They enjoy getting their own way in areas ranging from music to missions to church buildings, all the while heading toward burnout or contributing to the burnout of others. Like Diotrephes, they are often guilty of malicious words. Sometimes they cover their power struggles under the guise of church discipline and kick those who disagree with them out of the church. That was the course of action Diotrephes followed (3 John 10). The apostle John makes it clear two verses later that our course of action is not to mimic that which is evil, such as Diotrephes, but rather that which is good. In language similar to 2 Peter 1:9 John implies that the individual who acts like Diotrephes is spiritually nearsighted and does not see God accurately.

Perhaps it would be helpful at this point to examine which of the three areas—lust of the flesh (sexual or other physical temptation), lust of the eyes (material temptation), or pride of life (power struggle temptation)—is your most persistent struggle. If you are an obsessive-compulsive, it is likely that you are vulnerable to material temptation or power struggles, although you are susceptible to all three.

Take time to develop a plan of action to overcome these temptations. This plan may involve a daily time spent in prayer and in the Word. We have found in our personal experience that the discipline of a daily quiet time spent with God can be extremely crucial. Some find it helpful to have this quiet time either immediately before or immediately after a period of physical exercise, combining physical exercise and spiritual devotions on a regular basis.

THE INNER LIFE

The palm tree is one of the most resourceful and durable of plants. Unlike ordinary trees, which have dead centers and thinning roots, the palm's survival depends on a thick, strong root and living heart rather than on the condition of its leaves and bark. That is why the palm can withstand much external abuse. It endures violent desert storms by bending its resilient trunk until the rains and winds pass, after which the palm springs back. Its thick, strong root taps nearby streams or ponds for nourishment. Even if those resources dry up, the palm can still survive because the root, which is the same size as the trunk, stores a great surplus of water. In time (up to fifty years) the palm begins to bear fruit, which becomes sweeter as the palm tree ages and as its bark is scarred by the elements.

Like the palm tree, we endure when we tap into the resources of God's Spirit and His Word to develop the inner rather than the outer part of us. Psalm 1:2-4 tells us that the man is "blessed" whose "delight is in the law of the Lord, and [who meditates] on his law . . . day and night. He is like a tree planted by streams of water, which yields its fruit in season and whose leaf does not wither. Whatever he does prospers." We will bear fruit, all kinds of good deeds, and will grow spiritually as we get to know God better and better. God's power will strengthen us so that we can endure life's hardships joyfully (Colossians 1:11). Furthermore, we bear fruit also as we constantly give thanks for the eternal inheritance toward which we are advancing (vv. 10-12). When that happens, our daily lives will begin to demonstrate the divine difference. And, like Moses, we will constantly endure by seeing Him who is invisible.

11
SOLVING OUR
RELATIONAL PROBLEMS

Living a balanced, healthy life is not something that can be achieved in isolation. No less an authority than Dr. Karl Menninger, who has been described as knowing more about the subject of mental health than any other living person, offers the following perspective on a mentally healthy individual:

> Indeed, when we wish to find out how well Mr. X is integrated, we do not check his performance randomly at any odd level and leave it at that, but we try to formulate an organized statement about his overall functioning with an ultimate emphasis on his topmost performances: how he gets along with other people, how "whole" he is, how well he can adapt himself to the demands of the day, how well he can master his inner and outer environment to the benefit of himself and society.[1]

Many centuries before, Jesus Christ offered a perspective that provided His hearers with a way to evaluate overall human functioning; one that encompassed certain aspects of Menninger's perspective, but that,

1. Karl Menninger, *The Vital Balance* (New York: Viking Press, 1963), p. 94.

significantly, included another element—the vertical relationship with man's Creator.

Near the end of His ministry, after successfully responding to the Pharisees' and Sadducees' hostile questions, Jesus was confronted by a scribe who asked the question that many have wrestled with philosophically and theologically through the ages: "Of all the commandments, which is the most important?" (Mark 12:28). In other words, divinely speaking, what is our ultimate responsibility?

Without hesitation the Savior replied, "The most important one . . . is this: 'Hear, O Israel, the Lord our God, the Lord is one. Love the Lord your God with all your heart and with all your soul and with all your mind and with all your strength.' The second is this: 'Love your neighbor as yourself'" (Mark 12:29-31).

In essence, the Savior was saying that our ultimate responsibility is to love—to wholeheartedly love God and unconditionally love people. And He classified this responsibility as of overwhelming importance: "There is no commandment greater than these" (Mark 12:31*b*).

Sadly, however, twenty centuries later an endorsed definition of mental health conspicuously omits the relevance of those commandments. Menninger, a popular expert of our time, doesn't acknowledge that having a wholehearted love for God and for people is the key to developing lasting relationships and maintaining mental health.

Relating to others is often a difficult area for the burnout-prone obsessive-compulsive. However, before focusing on human relationships, it is necessary to be able to relate appropriately to God.

WHOLEHEARTED LOVE FOR GOD

The Pharisees of Jesus' day catalogued the law into 248 positive commandments and 365 prohibitions. They engaged in frequent debate about which laws took precedence over others in cases of apparent conflict.

In contrast, Jesus explained that the total responsibility of man can be summed up in one word—love. This is the essence of Paul's assertion in Romans 13:10, "Love is the fulfillment of the law."

Examination of the term *agape*, the Greek word Jesus used for love, shows us that love is not simply an emotion but an act of the will. It involves a choice to make someone or something else a priority rather than ourselves. Agape love gives sacrificially and desires the very best for the one loved.

The initial direction of this love is toward God. Jesus prefaced His answer to the scribe's question by quoting the most familiar verse of the Old Testament, one quoted frequently in Hebrew religious practice, "Hear, O Israel: The Lord our God, the Lord is one" (Deuteronomy 6:4). That verse stresses the uniqueness of God—only He deserves our wholehearted love.

Furthermore, Jesus explained that every part of man's being is to be involved in this expression of wholehearted love toward God. We prefer the phrase *wholehearted* love, not only because it is accurate in terms of Jesus' original statement, but also because it contrasts sharply with the halfhearted commitment in our world today.

According to Proverbs 4:23, the heart was the hub and center of man's existence, the ultimate source of every thought, every word, and every deed. We are to use our *soul* (emotions and attitudes), our *mind* (intellect and thought processes), and our *strength* (physical energies and efforts) *to love God.* In short, Jesus was saying that our total being is to be committed in a relationship of loving submission to God.

Paul may well have had this foundation in mind as he approached the close of his letter to the Thessalonians: "May God himself, the God of peace, sanctify you through and through. May your *whole—spirit, soul and body—*be kept blameless at the coming of our Lord Jesus Christ" (1 Thessalonians 5:23, author's emphasis and punctuation). This love is also based clearly on God's initiative of love toward us (1 John 4:19): "We love because he first loved us."

Two implications for burnout-prone obsessive-compulsives are evident from this discussion. First, the ultimate foundation for proper relationships is an understanding and appreciation of God's unconditional love for us. When we respond with wholehearted love for God, we are doing so not in attempts to win His approval or love but in recognition that He loves us totally and unconditionally. We don't have to earn or merit His love, but can simply respond to it wholeheartedly.

Second, our commitment is to a Person, not to a series of projects. Rather than being committed to projects that we think will earn God's favor, we need to be committed to God as a Person.

As we saw earlier, Martha is the classic biblical example of an individual committed to projects instead of persons. She was apparently an oldest daughter, someone who wanted to get things done and someone who apparently found it difficult to sit still. Her motto may well have been "Do it now!" She wasn't afraid of becoming involved physically in serving others (John 11:30). She was a strong thinker, even theologically, compared to many women of her day (v. 24), but she seemed to relate to Jesus on a level of something less than that of Lord, even to the point of admonishing Him (v. 39). Positively, of course, she sought out the Lord (v. 20), demonstrated a strong faith (v. 22), and had an accurate doctrinal framework of belief (vv. 24, 27).

Like many obsessive-compulsives, Martha seemed to be preoccupied with dirt, time, and money. In Luke 10 she is concerned with getting the housework done; in John 11 she questions why the Lord delayed His coming; and later in the passage she even voices her concern over the degree of decomposition of her brother's body! (v. 39). She was probably concerned about money, too, since the home she, Mary, and Lazarus lived in was hers (Luke 10:38). In essence, Martha was a high-performance individual who operated on a performance basis, even with God's Son.

What does it take to get through to someone like Martha? How could she change her project orientation to a wholehearted love for God? Perhaps the most significant statement in the entire New Testament about this special individual is found in John 11:5: "Jesus loved Martha and her sister and Lazarus." Jesus' unconditional love for Martha prompted Him to communicate with her, even though she seemed to have trouble listening to Him (vv. 23-27).

In fact, both in this context and in Luke 10, Martha tried to give the Lord advice, something we ourselves tend to do from time to time. Patiently, our Lord called her name twice, "Martha, Martha" (Luke 10:41), graciously and lovingly pointing out to her the ultimate priority of loving fellowship with Him. The Savior did not take away her desire to serve, however. In fact, in our final scriptural snapshot of Martha (John 12:2), she is still serving.

The highlight of this passage in John takes place at the celebration of Lazarus's restoration to life, where

Mary pours costly perfume on Jesus' feet in an act of worship. It is significant that when Judas Iscariot voices criticism of the wastefulness of Mary's act (John 12:4), we read nothing of criticism from Martha. Perhaps in response to Christ's unconditional love for her, Martha had come into a place of such wholehearted love for Him that a costly sacrificial act of worship, such as the one initiated by her sister, no longer created a practical problem for her.

Many obsessive-compulsives can relate to Martha's attempts to obtain God's favor on a performance basis. Such individuals usually become irritated with other people who hamper their efforts to perform. Obsessive-compulsives can learn from Martha's example as one who did respond to the unconditional love of Christ.

UNCONDITIONAL LOVE FOR PEOPLE

The second half of our ultimate responsibility that Christ describes to the scribe in Mark 12 is that we show unconditional love for people (v. 31). It is in our interactions with people that we will ultimately succeed in the abundant life Christ came to give us or sink into the mire of unfulfilled expectations that lead to burnout.

Because God loves us unconditionally and, as the Savior explains, because unconditional love for people is the hallmark of discipleship (John 15:12), it stands to reason that a proper response to God will result in an appropriately loving response towards people. As John expressed it, "Anyone who does not love his brother, whom he has seen, cannot love God, whom he has not seen" (1 John 4:20). Obsessive-compulsives who think they are wholly devoted to God but who struggle to show wholehearted love for family members, neighbors, coworkers, and church members are in for a surprise when they realize that their love for God is expressed by their love for other people.

Jesus said that we are to love our neighbors—those with whom we come in contact—as we love ourselves. Note that we are not commanded to love ourselves. Such love is assumed, just as it was assumed by the apostle Paul (Ephesians 5:28) when he explained that husbands are to love and cherish their wives as they do their own bodies.

Throughout the New Testament the priority of love is clearly established (Colossians 3:14; 1 Peter 4:8; 1 John 3:14; 1 John 4:8). Furthermore, every appropriate interpersonal relationship can be summarized in the essence of love, as described by Paul in 1 Corinthians 13:4-7*a*:

> Love is very patient and kind, never jealous or envious, never boastful or proud, never haughty or selfish or rude. Love does not demand its own way. It is not irritable or touchy. It does not hold grudges and will hardly even notice when others do it wrong. It is never glad about injustice, but rejoices whenever truth wins out. If you love someone you will be loyal to him no matter what the cost. [TLB*]

That is how we are to relate to the people God allows to cross our path. That includes members of our family, people with whom we work, believers with whom we worship and fellowship, and neighbors with whom we come in contact. We're to unconditionally love people not on the basis of how well they measure up to our conditions or how likable they are or how kind they are to us, but as the ultimate, outward expression of our inward commitment to Christ.

* *The Living Bible.*

We have noticed that people who unconditionally love their neighbor are almost immune to burnout and its complications, in contrast to the school bus driver mentioned earlier who deeply loved his bus—his material "possession." He was extremely fond of his route and the drive each day, and yet hated each one of the children who rode his bus.

Love does not mean the absence of conflict or confrontation. When Martha inappropriately rebuked our Lord, He gently and lovingly confronted her, pointing out her misplaced priorities (Luke 10:41-42). On another occasion He redirected her misplaced focus regarding her brother's future. Love may involve confrontation, yet frequently we fail to solve interpersonal conflicts through loving confrontation. Instead we choose to dwell on unmet expectations. That only leads to bitterness and eventually to burnout.

Even the apostle Paul encountered difficulty as a result of unrealistic expectations. After the Jerusalem council, in which Paul and Barnabas determined to undertake a second missionary journey (Acts 15:36), a major contention arose over the question of whether to take John Mark. Although Luke's account does not place blame on either Barnabas or Paul, or defend or censure John Mark for his earlier defection in Pamphylia, we learn that Paul had evidently expected a greater measure of commitment from John Mark than the young man was able to give. Paul even broke fellowship with Barnabas over this issue. Later, however, in 2 Timothy 4, as Paul expresses his concern over others who have abandoned him, such as Demas, he exhorts Timothy, "Get Mark and bring him with you, because he is helpful to me in my ministry" (2 Timothy 4:11). Paul gave us an encouraging example by extending a second opportunity to John Mark, instead of writing him off because he failed once to fulfill expectations.

That is an important example for us to follow when it comes to our unconditional love for people. They may sometimes fail us, and when they do, we may be inclined to become embittered and not to trust them with important responsibilities. Yet it is crucial not to write off people. Our God is the God of the second chance.

Paul is a good example of balance. Even though in writing to Timothy (2 Timothy 4), he cited many potential reasons to become bitter—toward Demas for forsaking him, toward Alexander for doing him harm, and toward other friends for deserting him to become involved in other ministries—Paul refused to follow what might have been his obsessive-compulsive tendency. He looked out for others and developed proper relationships, taking time to greet his long-time friends Priscilla, Aquila, and Onesiphorus, and allowing Trophimus to rest when he became ill.

Paul was able to maintain balance because he held onto a perspective that looked beyond the temporal to the eternal. Even though he experienced loneliness (2 Timothy 4:11), he recognized that the Lord's presence was with him. He even asked Timothy to come and be with him "before winter" (v. 21). Furthermore, Paul didn't suppress his emotions. He verbalized to Timothy his feelings about the fact that no one defended him at his first hearing (v. 16). Yet he was willing to forgive those who had deserted him and prayed that they would experience God's forgiveness.

BITTERNESS AND FORGIVENESS

This brings us to the issue of forgiveness. When others have failed to meet our expectations, why do we so frequently become bitter toward them? Often it is because we do not practice or understand the concept

of forgiveness. If bitterness is the hidden root of burnout, then forgiveness is the antidote that enables us to
move beyond burnout to abundant living. Often when
we encounter individuals who are overwhelmed by
burnout, it turns out that the source is primarily bitterness occasioned by a refusal to forgive others.

The meaning of the term *forgive* in both the Old
Testament and the New Testament is "to release" or
"send away." In fact, to forgive is to exercise a choice.
In his excellent work on the subject *Let's Forgive and
Be Free*, Richard Walters defines forgiving as "giving
up all claim on one who has hurt you and letting go of
the emotional consequences of the hurt" ([Grand Rapids: Zondervan, 1983] p. 18).

Several key New Testament passages articulate
crucial principles we need to understand relative to
forgiveness. Ephesians 4:32 explains the *degree* to
which we are to forgive—"just as in Christ God forgave
[us]." The *scope* of forgiveness is explained in Colossians 3:13: "Bear with each other and forgive *whatever* grievances you may have against one another"
(emphasis added). Romans 12:17-21 expresses the *essence* of forgiveness: "Do not repay anyone evil for evil.
Be careful to do what is right in the eyes of everybody.
If it is possible, as far as it depends on you, live at
peace with everyone. Do not take revenge, my friends,
but leave room for God's wrath, for it is written: 'It is
mine to avenge; I will repay,' says the Lord."

When we forgive, we are backing off and saying to
God, "If vengeance is to be taken, if a score is to be
settled, I'll let You take care of it. I give up the right to
pay back anybody. I want to do what is right and use
whatever power I have to get along with others."

The numerical *extent* of forgiveness is found in Jesus' statement to Peter—seventy times seven (Matthew
18:21-22). In other words, don't count or limit the

number of times you forgive. The *priority* of forgiving is expressed in Matthew 6:14-15. When we who desperately need God's forgiveness claim it but are unwilling to extend forgiveness to those who have wronged us, we will not experience divine forgiveness. Furthermore, the *consequences* of not forgiving can be seen in Ephesians 4:31-32. When we refuse to forgive, we harbor bitterness.

Characteristic symptoms of bitterness include rage, outbursts of anger, brawling, shouting, clamoring, slander (speaking evil of people), and malice (feelings of ill will). Those characteristics are magnified when we refuse to forgive. Furthermore, refusal to forgive will hinder us from being kind or tenderhearted. We are to be kind, or *chrestoi*, which according to *The Bible Knowledge Commentary* means to provide what is suitable or fitting to a need (ed. John F. Walvoord and Roy B. Zuck, New Testament ed. [Wheaton, Ill.: Victor Books, 1983], p. 637).

The term translated "tenderhearted" (KJV) is used only here in Ephesians and in 1 Peter 3:8, although a similar term is used in several of Paul's other letters and in 1 John 3:17. The basic idea is that the individual who is forgiving will maintain emotional and spiritual tenderness, instead of developing what might be called a "hard edge." Just as calluses can develop on a person's hands, so individuals who refuse to forgive, and harbor feelings of ill will, resentment, and bitterness, can become "hard-hearted." Obsessive-compulsive individuals, who tend to avoid relating on an emotional level, often struggle in this area. Yet the consequences of refusing to forgive are far too grave to neglect.

Forgiveness is neither cheap nor easy. Yet we try to avoid that reality, falling at times into certain traps. One of those traps is to forgive without dealing with the issue. We counseled a pastor whose son had become involved in all kinds of problems, including drugs and stealing. The father was always willing to forgive, but he never really faced head-on the reality of his son's destructive behavior.

Similarly, a wife who sought our counsel claimed to forgive her husband, who had been unfaithful. But she forgave him conditionally. As long as her husband treated her perfectly and provided everything that she wanted materially, she "forgave" him his infidelity. But inside she still harbored smoldering resentment. For years that greatly affected her relationship with her husband.

Another forgiveness trap is suppressing anger rather than forgiving. One man had supposedly forgiven his business partner for making a mistake in a business deal that cost the company thousands of dollars. But the man found himself taking out his anger and frustrations on his partner in little ways. It took years before he realized that, rather than completely forgiving him, he had forgiven only to a degree and for the most part had simply suppressed the rest of his anger.

A third trap is when we allow people to continue to hurt us. Matthew 10:16 instructs us to be wise as serpents and as innocent as doves. When we forgive another person, we must not harm him, just as a dove never attacks. But we must also exercise the wisdom of a serpent, which never places its head on the path where somebody is about to stomp with his boot. Serpents are shy creatures who avoid confrontation. When they are cornered they may attack out of self-defense, yet the normal nature of the serpent is to simply stay away. The safest way to deal with snakes is to make enough noise as you approach so that they have an opportunity to leave the area before you get close to them.

Forgiveness doesn't mean condoning wrong. It presupposes that the issue has been dealt with, just as God forgives our sins because their price has been paid with the death of His Son. Does this mean we forget when we forgive? No. Our computerlike brains have an incredible capability for remembering, even though emotionally we sometimes block out painful things that have happened to us. The memory of painful experiences remains present, frequently existing in layer after layer.

So how do we forgive? Scripture clearly states that we are to forgive before sunset, which was bedtime in the first-century (Ephesians 4:26). However, sometimes we think we've thoroughly forgiven only to wake up the next day to persisting anger. Often, forgiveness involves a commitment to the process of dealing with bitterness over and over again, whenever it flares up. It's like peeling an onion. We peel back a layer only to discover another. We deal with that layer only to discover another. It's a painful process filled with tears and pain. We forgive at great cost to ourselves. Yet the goal is to continue to deal with the issues until the emotional pain no longer exists, and the onion is completely peeled away.

In some situations that will take intensive counseling and require that we will to make difficult choices. But if we are to appropriately, unconditionally love people, we have to forgive them.

Can we forgive? Yes. Why? Because God, for Christ's sake, has forgiven us. Think of all the ways God has forgiven us. He has blotted out like a thick cloud our transgressions (Isaiah 44:22); He has removed our sins "as far as the east is from the west" (Psalm

103:12); and He pardons sin and has hurled our ini-
quities into the depth of the sea (Micah 7:18-19).

Will we forgive? Ultimately we must make that
choice. To choose to forgive whether we feel like it or
not is an essential prerequisite for moving beyond
burnout.

12
RELATING POSITIVELY TO OTHERS

Recently a young man appeared in our office to interview for a job opening in a new clinic that was being established in a nearby city. During the course of the interview, he asserted, "Here's how I operate. Give me a job to do, and I'll do it. I'm the kind of person who likes to know what's expected of me, to whom I'm responsible, and how soon I need to get a job done. If there's one phrase that characterizes me it's, 'I am responsible.' "

The two of us present with the young man looked at each other and smiled as we thought the same thing, "Ah ha! Another obsessive-compulsive personality!"

Since this book is written about balancing obsessive-compulsive traits (which are not bad in themselves), it is important to recognize that one of the major strengths of the obsessive-compulsive is his conscientiousness about duty—a positive trait to have in the Christian life, for God has given us some important responsibilities to fulfill.

As we learn from Jesus in Mark 12:30-31, our ultimate duty is not a responsibility toward projects but toward persons. It is to love God wholeheartedly and to love people unconditionally. "Love the Lord your God with all your heart and with all your soul and with all your mind and with all your strength. The second is this: Love your neighbor as yourself. There is no commandment greater than these."

In the previous chapter, we examined some problem areas relating to our responsibility to love our neighbor. In this chapter, we shall seek to move beyond correcting the negative by addressing the positive. In addition, we will seek to present workable principles for building and maintaining positive relationships.

As we try to relate to others on the basis of unconditional love, we quickly find that forgiving isn't enough. We also have a strong need to develop positive relationships to which we can contribute and which will encourage and strengthen us. The book of Proverbs contains a great deal of wisdom about relationships. Much of that wisdom comes from Solomon, who learned it firsthand from his father, David.

Perhaps the classic example of a healthy interpersonal relationship can be seen in the friendship between David and Jonathan. A superficial examination of that unique and special relationship demonstrates that good friends don't have to come from the same social status. Jonathan was a prince and David only a poor shepherd, and Jonathan may have been fifteen to twenty years older than David. The biblical narrative in 1 Samuel tells us that this special relationship developed shortly after David's dramatic victory over Goliath. The record states: "The soul of Jonathan was knit to the soul of David, and Jonathan loved him as himself" (18:1, NASB*).

How could such a special relationship of love develop? The Hebrew word *aheb*, used for love, is one of two key words that describe relationships in the Old Testament. As a noun, it describes one who loves or one who is a friend. For example, it describes Abraham in

* *New American Standard Bible.*

2 Chronicles 20:7 and in Isaiah 41:8 as a friend of God. It denotes a choice, an attraction, and a camaraderie, which is seen in the process of "knitting of souls" between David and Jonathan.

From a human perspective, why did this friendship occur? It occurred because even though Jonathan and David came from different backgrounds, they had the same determination and spirit regarding God's purposes and victory over God's enemies. David had just demonstrated that attitude by his willingness to take on the giant Goliath, something the other warriors of Israel had been unable or unwilling to do. Somewhat earlier, Jonathan had demonstrated the same attitude, telling his armor-bearer, "Perhaps the Lord will act in our behalf. Nothing can hinder the Lord from saving, whether by many or by few" (1 Samuel 14:6). God used a courageous, responsive Jonathan and his armor-bearer to dispatch about twenty men across a half-acre of ground and to initiate an even greater victory as a result of a supernaturally timed earthquake, which terrorized the Philistines. "So the Lord rescued Israel that day" (v. 23).

The similarities between Jonathan's actions and attitude in 1 Samuel 14 and David's in 1 Samuel 17 are remarkable. Both realized they were facing tremendous odds, yet both recognized the power of God to overcome those odds. Each verbalized a personal faith and confidence in God, acted on that faith, and, as a result, each experienced victory. Their commitment to God and their attitudes toward life and struggles bonded them.

In seeking friendships we should look for people who realistically assess the difficulties of life but whose faith and confidence in God are genuine and strong; people who, rather than hindering or dragging down our faith, will encourage it or promote it; people who will stimulate our spiritual growth rather than retard it. We should look for people whose attitudes toward the things of God are positive rather than negative.

In addition to having similar attitudes toward God, David and Jonathan also exhibited a similar commitment to their friendship in the making of a covenant (1 Samuel 18:3). We're living in days when people are slack in making and keeping commitments to one another. In our culture of "least resistance" we often apply an attitude of convenience toward our relationships as well, expecting to start and stop a friendship whenever we feel like it. As a result, we lose out on the benefits of long-term commitments. Many marriages fail today because individuals base the marriage on short-term physical attraction or emotions and don't want to spend time and effort developing a substantial friendship and commitment within the marriage.

The Old Testament concept of commitment is fascinating. It signifies loyal love and refers to an important long-term relationship of the type exhibited by Jonathan and David. The concept of loyal love (referred to twice regarding their friendship) provided the basis for a covenant relationship between them (1 Samuel 20:14-15).

Even though Jonathan was next in line to the throne of Israel, and even though his father pressured him to turn against David and to pursue his own interests, Jonathan remained loyal to David—defending him to the point of risking his own life for his friend (1 Samuel 19:1-5, 20:30-34). The idea of loyalty is also mentioned in 20:15: "Do not ever cut off your kindness from my family." Jonathan even reaffirmed his oath to David, "because he loved him as he loved himself" (v. 17). The love and loyalty in this covenant were possible because the relationship was actually a three-sided one among David, Jonathan, and the Lord (v. 8). God blesses relationships that honor Him. Developing long-term, committed relationships that have the common priority of glorifying God helps us to grow closer to the Lord and prepares us to be an instrument He can use to care for and bless others.

Philip and Dick were college roommates who often played basketball together and double-dated together. After both graduated from college, they went their separate ways for five years without seeing one another. Yet each often thought of and even prayed for the other.

One spring, Philip's business took him to the Midwest where Dick was involved in a ministry. Certain about how he felt toward his old friend, but uncertain as to how he would be received, Philip decided to risk a phone call. Dick was ecstatic. The two men had lunch and Dick invited Philip to visit his family. As a result, both men verbalized their disappointment in themselves for allowing time and the pressures of life to erode their commitment to keep in contact.

Philip said, "Why don't you plan on bringing your family and spending some vacation time with us on the East Coast?" The two families spent a week together, and the ease with which the relationship was reestablished confirmed the genuine long-term commitment between Philip and Dick.

Have you ever been out of touch with old friends for years only to get back together and realize that the relationship is just as strong and solid as ever? If so, that friendship likely involved a long-term commitment. To verbalize such a commitment to a friend by saying, "I'm committed to you," "I care about you," or "I'm with you for the long haul" is appropriate and provides tremendous encouragement, support, and hope for friends who are experiencing adversity.

A committed relationship also involves a genuine delight and enjoyment in the success of the other. That was especially evident in Jonathan's attitude toward David. The scriptural record zeros in on Jonathan's delight in David's success, in contrast with Saul's extreme jealousy toward David (1 Samuel 18:8). Jonathan gave David a robe, kingly garments, sword, bow, and belt (v. 4); he defended David to his father (19:4-5); he communicated with David in order to restore him to Saul's household (v. 7); he encouraged David when David focused on the unfairness and the hopelessness of his deteriorating relationship with Saul (23:17), and even took personal risk to do so in the wilderness (vv. 16-18) where he reaffirmed his commitment to God's ultimate purpose, which was to establish David as king. Jonathan physically and verbally expressed appropriate affection toward his friend (20:41-42). Jonathan not only expressed his commitment to David (vv. 9-17) but even grieved for David because of the rift in the relationship between his father and his friend (v. 34).

Not everything in this friendship was praiseworthy, however. Jonathan lied on behalf of his friend (20:28), something clearly prohibited by the Scriptures, even when the falsehood grows out of a desire to be loyal to our friends. But overall the friendship was one we should emulate. There was no jealousy in the relationship but genuine, open communication and an unselfish, giving spirit. Possessiveness and self-seeking found no place, nor were the emotions of anger, bitterness, or envy allowed to pollute the positive qualities of the relationship.

As David experienced the benefits of developing a good friendship, he was able to communicate to his son Solomon the principles of friendship he had experienced in his dealings with Jonathan. Unfortunately,

Solomon did not practice everything he learned or even everything he taught in the book of Proverbs. Yet he established some important principles of relationships, which we need to apply.

One of those principles is found in Proverbs 13:20: "He who walks with the wise grows wise, but a companion of fools suffers harm." This principle relates to marriages, friendships, work relationships, and even relationships within the local church. Those who have allowed God to develop wisdom in them through His Word and their life experiences can help strengthen and enhance the wisdom of others. Yet our personal lives will be "broken down" (the literal meaning of the Hebrew word *yeroa*), harmed, and destroyed if we spend our time with and choose as friends those who have a foolish attitude toward life.

A classic biblical example of someone who chose the wrong kind of friends was Joash (2 Chronicles 24). Spurning the counsel of his wise guardian, Jehoiada, he chose foolish friends from among the princes of Judah—friends who instigated the murder of Jehoiada's son, Zechariah (2 Chronicles 24:21-22).

As has already been mentioned, the kind of relationships or friendships we develop can play a crucial role in determining whether we flourish in life or experience the bitterness that often leads to burnout. A key relationship principle is espoused in Proverbs 17:17, "A friend loves at all times, and a brother is born for adversity." Jonathan loved David even when he faced the loss of the privilege of becoming king, just as Joseph continued to love and care for his brothers, even after they had sold him into slavery.

Proverbs 18:24b tells us that "there is a friend who sticks closer than a brother." Some translations of the first part of Proverbs 18:24 suggest that a lot of friends can be destructive, but a few good, close, loyal friends can help. An authentic friend is one who knows you at your best and worst and still loves and accepts you.

Proverbs 27 contains a number of highly significant principles related to friendships. Proverbs 27:5-6 states that "open rebuke" is "better . . . than hidden love. Wounds from a friend can be trusted, but an enemy multiplies kisses." We need faithful friends—friends who can be trusted to tell us the truth. We may be tempted to surround ourselves with people who only flatter us, who only tell us what we want to hear. But a genuine friend is one who will tell us the truth even when it wounds us.

A pastor was investing far too much time in work and in ministry. Although many people said, "What you're doing is great. You must be really having an effect for Christ," a few close friends said, "What you're doing is destructive. It ultimately will cause you to lose your health and the ability to minister five or ten years down the road." Even though the words were painful, the pastor needed them.

The New Testament encourages us to admonish one another. Appropriate confrontation is far better than a "Judas kiss." A true friend tells it like it is in contrast to the flatterer, who may cause us to stumble. "Whoever flatters his neighbor is spreading a net for his feet" (Proverbs 29:5). A true friend faithfully comforts as well as confronts. "Ointment and perfume rejoice the heart; so doth the sweetness of a man's friend by hearty counsel" (Proverbs 27:9, KJV).

The Israelites lived in a hot, dry climate. So oil on the skin provided a soothing, refreshing balm, and perfume stimulated the senses and encouraged appreciation for the finer things of life. So it is with the encouragement and comfort of a good friend. None of us can be "up" all the time. We all need "counsel from the heart," the kind of encouragement a friend can give.

The book of Proverbs has a lot to say about the subject of counsel or direction. Many people are unwilling to ask for it. Others ask the wrong person or fail to heed good advice. Proverbs tells us we all need "hearty counsel" from time to time. The Hebrew word used for counsel here is *tahbuloth*, which carries the basic idea of seeking direction. We've all tried to find a place we've never been to before and have needed to stop and ask for directions. The concept of seeking counsel is the same. The word *tahbuloth* is used five times in Proverbs (1:5, 11:14, 12:5, 20:18, and 24:6). Its root is related to a nautical word for a rope that is pulled to steer a ship.

Proverbs 11:14 states, "For lack of guidance a nation falls, but many advisers make victory sure," pointing out that when counsel isn't present, a group of people is likely to fall. The context of this verse suggests people, relations, and activities possibly within a city or community (vv. 10-11), although the advice can apply also to individuals. Yet, security in each case comes from "a multitude of counselors." The idea is that ensuring safety or security requires skill in making decisions. The concept of utilizing many advisers, found in Proverbs 11:14, 15:22, and 24:6, carries the idea of our seeking a second opinion. We should not simply limit ourselves to the counsel of one friend or individual, just as we should not always depend on the opinion of one physician. One of the reasons God gave us two eyes is because perception and perspective are improved with two eyes rather than with only one. Similarly, it is far safer to utilize the perspective of two or more persons.

Proverbs 15:22 gives a similar perspective: "Plans fail for lack of counsel, but with many advisers they succeed." Here the issue is not simply safety but success and fulfillment in life. Earlier, the author of Proverbs contrasted a wise son who brings joy to his father with a foolish son who thinks little of his parents. Without counsel, purposes will come to naught. We may plan as we wish, but we may experience disappointment if they are made foolishly.

In the years following the oil bust in Texas, hundreds of new, empty office buildings in Dallas, Austin, and Houston lined the landscape. Each of those buildings represented plans and purposes that had been disappointed. Every week the newspapers carried column after column of new bankruptcy declarations, many of well-known, previously wealthy people.

However, there were individuals who were able to maintain fiscal stability and success during that time. Such a man was Jim, a banker who had been involved in oil and real estate investments. He was advised by two individuals to diversify and to exercise caution before going into projects during the years when the oil decline first affected the economy. Because he listened to his advisers, Jim experienced a personal and financial stability not experienced by many of his peers. Counsel heeded led to success. Jim was a living example of the truth of Proverbs 20:18, "Make plans by seeking advice; if you wage war, obtain guidance."

Proverbs 24:6 gives similar counsel. "For waging war you need guidance, and for victory many advisers." The context of the verse is strength and stability (see vv. 3-5), and the subject is an impending conflict or a developing war. Conflict is a common aspect of life; it often occurs among families, in business, and even in the church. The principle of Proverbs 24:6 applies not only to presidents, such as John F. Kennedy facing the Bay of Pigs, or Ronald Reagan dealing with Libyan leader Moammar Khadafy, but also to us when we face conflict at home, in church, and at work. Those are the times we need to seek counsel.

A church faced a major conflict over whether or not to build a new building. Even though the members had long agreed that a new building should be constructed, an offer for a different, free location for the new church building created controversy. Some members saw the new location as a great blessing and opportunity, but others remained loyal to the church's location of the past thirty years. The conflict threatened to split the church. The pastor sought counsel from the elders in the church, from other experienced pastors in the area, and from church leaders in other parts of the country. After seeking a multitude of counselors, the pastor and the elders devised a plan for harmony. Ultimately, the plan worked to pull together the congregation, and, although some members did leave the congregation, the number was far less than it could have been. Those who stayed worked together and saw the new facility constructed. And the church's growth and its outreach in the community continued in an even larger measure.

Everyone needs friends from whom they can seek open counsel—friends who will give them encouragement and friends they can mutually stimulate and sharpen. Proverbs 27:17 states, "As iron sharpens iron, so one man sharpens another." That verse gives a vivid image of mutual intellectual and spiritual interaction and growth among friends. Occasionally such interaction as "iron sharpening iron" will cause sparks to fly. One of the best definitions we know for "encouraging one another" (Greek *parakaleo*, Hebrews 10:25) is to comfort the afflicted or to afflict the comfortable. This process of encouraging one another can help all of us. Some people leave very little impact on our lives, whereas others who encourage us make indelible impressions on us.

Another important principle of friendship demonstrated in Proverbs 27 is loyalty. "Do not forsake your friend and the friend of your father, and do not go to your brother's house when disaster strikes you" (v. 10). When adversity strikes, it's time to demonstrate loyalty to friends and to anticipate their loyalty toward us.

Tim was a section leader in a medium-sized corporation.. He and Harold, his department manager, had worked together for a number of years. They had started working for the company at the same time and had both worked their way up to management positions.

A new corporate vice-president was hired with whom Harold did not see eye to eye, and Tim was offered Harold's job without Harold's knowing it. Because of his loyalty to his friend, Tim turned down the offer. He knew Harold was a good manager and that the complaints of incompetence the new vice-president voiced about Harold had no basis. Turning down the position, however, almost cost Tim his job.

Ultimately, Harold quit the company and moved to another. He and Tim remained good friends. Tim was not promoted into Harold's old spot but, as he told a friend, "My friendship with Harold was a lot more important than the promotion, especially with what I would have had to do to get it. I believe Harold would have stuck with me if the shoe were on the other foot. I couldn't have faced myself in the mirror if I had done that to him."

Loyalty can include keeping issues between you and your friend without breaking confidences (Proverbs 25:9-10),˙or just saying the appropriate word of encouragement (v. 11) or a proper word of rebuke (v. 12). It includes verbally giving the right word of refreshment (v. 13) and not making promises that you cannot or will not fulfill (v. 14). Remember—loyalty and a close friendship don't mean we should presume on past times of intimacy. Proverbs 27:14 warns, "If a man loudly blesses his neighbor early in the morning, it will be taken as a curse." The principle in that verse is two-fold: (1) practice sincerity in verbal communication and be sensitive to a friend's feelings of the moment, and (2) know when to back off. Even close, loyal friends may need some distance at times.

We can see a classic example of appropriate friend-ship in the relationship we have with Jesus Christ and what He has done for us. The basis for our relationship with Him is His sacrificial love (John 15:13), which caused Him to lay down His life for us. The result of His love and friendship has changed us. We are trans-formed (v. 14), which leads to a close, personal intima-cy with Him and to a fruitfulness in our lives (v. 16). We no longer relate to Him simply as servants but as friends, which was the highest title that could be be-stowed by an oriental king.

Close examination of those verses gives us impor-tant principles to apply to friendships. For example: Do I have the kind of wholehearted commitment of love that Christ has for me? Am I willing to be open and to relate to others as friends rather than on a perfor-mance basis? Do I reach out to others as Christ did for me? Do I choose friends on the basis of my needs or on the basis of my willingness to give to them? Finally, are my friends becoming more like Christ and more effec-tively bearing fruit because of me?

We all need friends. Facing the most intense trial of His life—the cross—Jesus called out for Peter, James, and John in the Garden of Gethsemane and asked them to stay with Him (Mark 14:32-42). The apostle Paul, near the close of his life, wrote to Timothy about his loneliness and encouraged his friend to "come before winter" (2 Timothy 4:21, NASB). How are friends to treat each other? With encouragement, perhaps the most important principle in friendship.

The spiritual gift of exhortation or encouragement—the God-given ability to appropriately motivate another individual—is not the gift of manipulation, of arm-twisting, or of simply giving someone else "a piece of your mind." Exhortation or encouragement is described as a function of the Holy Spirit in John 14 and 16. Like the Holy Spirit, an encourager or exhorter is one who is called alongside another. The concept can include rebuking another, calling for a change of action (Philippians 4:2), giving positive encouragement and comfort (2 Corinthians 1:3-4, 2:6-8), or challenging an individual to take action (Romans 12:1, 15:30; Jude 3). Although encouragement can be either public or private, the private use of the function has particular significance for believers. For example, 1 Timothy 4:13 points out that church leaders are to practice encouragement, whether or not they have the gift, as are all believers (1 Thessalonians 4:18, 5:11; Hebrews 10:25).

Two individuals in the New Testament stand out as patterns for encouragement. One is Barnabas, who was given that name by the apostles. The term means "son of encouragement or exhortation." Several instances in his life, recorded in the book of Acts, show the ways Barnabas demonstrated himself to be an encourager. The first glimpse we have of this man shows him exercising generosity, using his financial resources to encourage fellow members of the Body of Christ (Acts 4:36-37). He generously and willingly gave of his personal resources in a sacrificial way, which starkly contrasted with Ananias and Sapphira, who made a show of complete giving but secretly held some back.

Later Barnabas encouraged young Saul of Tarsus, who had recently been converted to the Christian faith (9:27). When everybody else was afraid of Saul (because of his record of persecuting the church), Barnabas brought him to the apostles, declared his testimony, and attested to its truthfulness. Undoubtedly, Barnabas's loyalty, encouragement, and willingness to use his influence played a strategic role in shaping Saul's ministry. He was renamed Paul the apostle and became a champion of the faith.

The same personal loyalty in Barnabas led to a rift between Barnabas and Paul in Acts 15:37-39. Barnabas felt strongly inclined to give John Mark a second chance. As earlier observed, Scripture does not say who was right and who was wrong. The rift led to Paul and Barnabas going separate ways. In spite of their split, Scripture records that Barnabas and Paul were both used by God. Eventually, Paul extended a second chance to John Mark (2 Timothy 4:11). Perhaps that was a result of having recognized that attitude in Barnabas, who used forgiveness and a second chance as a tool for encouragement.

When the name of another biblical encourager is mentioned, it usually elicits the reaction, "Who's he?" Yet Paul recognized Onesiphorus as one of the most important encouragers in his life. Although he was probably dead by the time Paul wrote of him, Onesiphorus left a lasting legacy. Paul said, "He often refreshed me" (2 Timothy 1:16). The word he used for *refreshed* means "to lift up one's soul" and is used only here in the New Testament. It speaks of a striking act of encouragement.

Furthermore, when other people were embarrassed by Paul's incarceration for the cause of Christ, Onesiphorus was "not ashamed of [Paul's] chains" (v. 16*b*).

He sought Paul in Rome and found him. His efforts to find the apostle were not halfhearted attempts. He went the extra mile to make personal contact. And that was only a glimpse of his ministry of encouragement. Paul said to Timothy, "You know very well in how many ways he helped me in Ephesus" (v. 18). Onesiphorus had been like a personal servant to Paul, lifting his soul and bringing encouragement to him. In essence, he was the epitome of what relating to others should be. He left a lasting impact on Paul and provides a stellar example for us as well.

Onesiphorus illustrates a phrase seen on a greeting card: "Most smiles are started by another smile." How many smiles have you started? As obsessive-compulsives who have received conditional love, and as bitter victims of burnout, we may not be appropriately relating to others by initiating a chain of smiles. Yet, following the examples of Onesiphorus, Barnabas, David, Jonathan, Paul, Timothy, and others in the New Testament, we can choose to become the first link in an encouraging chain.

13

HANDLING THE CIRCUMSTANCES OF LIFE

Jesus Christ is our ultimate pattern. As we seek to learn from His example, several important characteristics stand out that we can emulate in His approach to life. Let's look more closely at these principles for living.

ESTABLISHING PURPOSE

First, every aspect of Jesus' life revolved around His purpose and mission. Throughout the gospels Jesus makes frequent reference to the will of "him who sent me" (cf. John 5:30). We see this early in His ministry, such as in His contact with the woman at the well and His subsequent explanation of that incident to the disciples, and in the discourse that followed His healing of the invalid at the pool of Bethesda.

When Jesus presented Himself to the multitudes as the true bread of life (John 6:35-40), He exhibited the same commitment to doing the will of God. In those verses John portrays Jesus as both human and divine in His personal relationship to God. Jesus explains that His reason for existing is to fulfill the will of the Father (v. 38). It is the will of God that drives Him to complete the work of salvation (v. 39). It is the will of

God that Jesus present Himself as Savior and pay the price for sin so that those who trust Him might have everlasting life (v. 40). Throughout John's gospel Jesus relates our doing God's will to assurance of salvation (7:17), genuine worship, and answer to prayer (9:31).

Jesus is our example in obeying God's will (Matthew 26:42). For Him, life was based on one consuming purpose—to obey His Father's wishes.

Yet His life revolved around that purpose in a balanced way. He took time to sleep, to eat meals, and to fellowship with friends (Luke 10:38). He found time to visit those who had personal needs (Luke 18). He encouraged His disciples to take time to rest and joined them in doing so (Mark 6:31). Still, whatever He did and planned centered on the purpose He Himself stated in Luke 19:10: "The Son of Man came to seek and to save what was lost" (NASB).

Just as Jesus did, we need to recognize that we are called of God, whether to vocational ministry or to personal service, and we need to gear our lives toward fulfilling that call and exercising balance in daily living.

ESTABLISHING PRIORITIES

The second principle, rooted in the first, is that Jesus demonstrated priority. The major focus of His time, as we observe in the gospels, was to train twelve men to carry on His work after He left. Perhaps we can best observe this focus in Jesus' conversation with His Father the night before the crucifixion. The conversation, recorded in John 17, is what may be called the "real" Lord's Prayer. In that passage Jesus gives perhaps the clearest outline of the process of discipleship. Although many books have been written about discipleship during the last half century, no one has improved on the manual for discipleship outlined in John 17. There Jesus tells us precisely how He invested His time in discipling others to carry on His work when His time on earth was completed.

In that prayer Jesus made several statements regarding His disciples, and each statement represented a component of discipleship. He considered those components of such high priority that He invested more time in training the twelve that He did in reaching the multitudes. Let's examine those six statements and the components they represent.

1. *Example*—"I have revealed you to those whom you gave me" (v. 6). Many Christians fail in discipleship because they forget that what they do speaks louder than what they say. Because Jesus was perfect, He didn't have that problem; we might, but we need to give evidence of spiritual maturity to those lives we would impact.

2. *Evangelism*—"I gave them the words you gave me" (v. 8). Jesus, extending the call to His disciples, offered them the gift of everlasting life. He personally drew each of them into faith in Him. Many mature Christians see evangelism as too basic, something in which only young, exuberant Christians should engage. Nothing could be further from the truth. Evangelism is the duty of *every* believer and is an intrinsic part of the process of discipleship.

3. *Endurance and encouragement*—"I protected them and kept them safe by that name you gave me" (v. 12). Clearly, we do not have the same ability today to keep people in Jesus' name that He had as a supernatural Savior. Yet, through endurance (not giving up) and encouragement (motivating those we disciple not

to give up), we can play a key role in keeping others from becoming spiritual casualties.

4. *Edification*—"I have given them your word" (v. 14). Here the consequent growth Jesus describes progresses to such an extent that the world sees the difference in those who are disciples of Jesus Christ. Later, in verse 17, Jesus adds, "Sanctify them by the truth; your word is truth." Teaching spiritual truth to disciples is commonly considered a key role of discipleship. We cannot have discipleship without the teaching-learning process, for it is inherent to discipleship. The gospels show that Jesus invested a great deal of His time teaching His disciples. We, too, need to be involved in teaching God's truth to those we disciple.

5. *Extension*—"I have sent them into the world" (v. 18). Ideally, the person who is discipling another should be training him to disciple others. As Jesus uttered this statement, He was less than twenty-four hours away from a dramatic separation from His disciples. In less than two months He would return to heaven and no longer be with them physically. We, also, need to prepare those we disciple for the time when they will be on their own—training them not to simply survive but to disciple others.

Today we see highly visible leaders drawing disciples after themselves. In his letter to the first-century church in Corinth, Paul pointed out the same tendency (1 Corinthians 1:12). Our priority in discipleship should be making disciples of Jesus Christ, not of ourselves or of other leaders. To the extent that we make disciples who follow Christ, we succeed; to the extent that we make disciples of other men, we fail. That is the standard that guided the apostle Paul: "Follow my example, as I follow the example of Christ" (1 Corinthians 11:1).

DEALING WITH INTERRUPTIONS

Jesus was able to handle interruptions, which provides us a third principle. Most of us are interrupted on many occasions, and frequently we do not handle those interruptions well. We may become distracted and lose sight of our purpose, or we may be so purposeful as to ignore the priorities of the persons who interrupt us. Our children, for example, frequently demand attention when we are busy with things we consider to be more important. Sometimes our immediate concerns *are* more important, but not always. When we see ourselves placing a newspaper article or the nightly television news above spending time with our children, we need to rethink our priorities.

The gospel of Mark provides many examples of Jesus handling interruptions well. After He healed a man with an unclean spirit (Mark 1:21-26), Jesus was suddenly interrupted by an entire city who demanded His attention (1:33). He was then interrupted in the midst of His teaching by four men carrying a paralyzed man (2:1-5); they let the man down through a hole in the flat roof of the building in which Jesus was teaching. Later Jesus was pursued and interrupted by a large multitude (3:7-9). At one point, after being interrupted by Jairus, a synagogue ruler whose daughter was at the point of death (5:22), Christ was almost immediately interrupted again by a woman with a long-term physical problem, an issue of blood (v. 25-29). The Savior compassionately handled all of those interruptions well. Later, en route to Jerusalem to die for the sins of the world, Christ responded to the insistent interruption of Bartimaeus, a blind beggar (10:46-52).

In examining these and other instances in which the Savior was interrupted, several important principles stand out that we can apply to our own lives. First,

Christ always responded graciously. He never conveyed the attitude that people did not have a right to interrupt Him. He was available. Second, He made people a priority. For the most part, those who interrupted Christ were not prominent individuals. Yet Christ treated them as important individuals, those for whom He had time and about whom He cared. Third, although He was frequently interrupted, Christ did not allow those interruptions to deflect Him from His ultimate purpose. For example, after dealing with the woman with the issue of blood, Christ immediately went on to raise Jairus's daughter from the dead. And after restoring Bartimaeus's sight, He immediately resumed His journey to Jerusalem. Fourth, on occasion the Savior actually initiated an interruption Himself. He interrupted His healing of the paralytic to point out the hardened unbelief in the hearts of some of His observers (Mark 2:8). Later, He interrupted His teaching of the multitude to call Levi the tax collector to follow Him (2:14). Fifth, when important priorities made it necessary, Christ isolated Himself from interruptions, for example, in the period immediately before His selection of the twelve disciples (3:13).

Learning to handle interruptions in a Christlike fashion will take us a significant distance down the road of handling life's circumstances.

PUTTING COMPETITION INTO PERSPECTIVE

Jesus never felt competitive. The Pharisees led obviously competitive lives, competing among themselves and with the Sadducees. Both of those groups competed with the Herodians and sought to compete with Jesus. Even Jesus' disciples competed with each other to see who would be the greatest in His kingdom (Matthew 18:1). The mother of Zebedee's sons asked Jesus to grant them the honor of sitting on either side of Him in the kingdom (Matthew 20:20-23). But our Savior was not interested in competing with anyone. For Him life was simply a matter of fulfilling the purpose and calling for which He had come.

ENSURING OUR CONTINUED GROWTH

Even though Jesus was the perfect Son of God, the Scriptures say He grew physically (stature), intellectually (wisdom), and socially (in favor with God and man). This is an extremely important principle for living. We must experience growth as well. According to Gail Sheehy, development is needed in three basic frontiers—our work, our relationships, and ourselves.

Perhaps it is this failure of continued growth that leads to spiritual bankruptcy and what we have come to call a mid-life crisis. Psychologist Daniel Levenson, in *U.S. News and World Report*, describes a mid-life crisis as a time when people question seriously their life patterns and goals. If we have invested time toward balanced growth, we are far less likely to experience a mid-life crisis than those individuals who fail to make those investments.

One of King David's life goals was to build a grand temple for worshiping God. Although he completed preparations for the project, he was not allowed to achieve his goal. Rather the task was completed by his son Solomon.

Many years later, while Israel was in captivity, Nehemiah learned of the destitution of Jerusalem and committed himself to rebuilding the walls and city. He invested prayer, courage, careful planning, and hard work. And he completed his goal.

The apostle Paul was motivated by the goal of proclaiming the gospel of Christ where others had never preached (Romans 15:14-22). That goal drove him from one end of the Roman Empire to the other and ultimately led to his imprisonment. Paul also had the goal of achieving spiritual maturity. Paul had both goals in mind when he wrote, "I press on toward the goal to win the prize for which God has called me heavenward in Christ Jesus" (Philippians 3:14).

Our goals and objectives need to be broken down into specific subgoals. Physical goals may involve exercise. The overarching goal of being physically fit may include specific targets concerning weight control and proper eating habits. The overarching goal of maintaining thriving interpersonal relationships may include a specific checklist having to do with developing friendships and spending time with one's spouse, children, and friends. The overarching goal of developing intellectual sharpness may include the subgoal of enrolling in academic courses and embarking on a personal reading program. The goal of developing spiritual maturity may include subgoals having to do with Bible reading, Scripture memorization, or participation in an advanced Bible study course.

Our goals need to be *attainable*. Unfortunately we tend to set our standards too high, particularly if we are perfectionists. Recently, a staff counselor at our clinic lost nearly fifty pounds within a year. For most of us, such a goal probably would not be attainable. We are often faced with a dilemma: what price are we willing to pay to achieve a specific goal and will the achievement of our goal create imbalance in other areas of our lives?

Our goals need to be *measurable*. It is of little value simply to plan to "pray more." Rather, you need to have a specific measure of both quantity and time. If you plan to pray ten minutes daily throughout the next year, you will know whether or not you are fulfilling your goal.

Our goals need to be *flexible*. This is particularly true for the obsessive-compulsive. It is easy for us to become so enmeshed in a specific goal that we feel like a total failure if we fail to reach that goal. Even worse, in the process of trying to meet one goal we may neglect other basic needs or the needs of those around us. Occasional mid-course corrections have been necessary of every manned venture into space; such should be incorporated into our lives as well.

We need to remember that growth is *not instant*. A few years ago one of the authors and his family moved into a house in a suburban community north of Dallas. In that subdivision houses were stacked row upon row. Each house had two "instant trees" planted in the front yard. Within the first three months his instant trees had to be replaced twice. However, in the backyard was a massive pecan tree that obviously had been around long before the subdivision. Many years before, a pecan had fallen to the ground and taken root, and from it sprouted a small, fragile tree that grew and withstood the elements. It drew nutrients from the soil, carbon dioxide from the air, and energy from the sunshine. Today it furnishes shelter, shade, beauty, and even the makings of an occasional pecan pie—all because it was allowed time to grow.

The author of Hebrews 5 expresses sorrow over the lack of growth in those to whom he is writing. Second Peter 3:18 exhorts us to "grow in the grace and knowledge of our Lord and Savior Jesus Christ." To grow in grace is the continuous expansion of the enablement He gives us through His indwelling Spirit. To grow in knowledge is the continued development of both the understanding and application of the truth of His Word. Both are essential to spiritual progress.

OUR IMMEDIATE PRIORITIES

What are some priorities of growth that we need to recognize as immediate needs?

CHARACTER DEVELOPMENT

Many people today emphasize only excellence in what they do. Scripture focuses more on character—what we *are*—for that is where God's concern lies. Over an extended period of time former Dallas Cowboys head coach Tom Landry has exhibited excellence of character. For most of that time his Dallas Cowboys succeeded, but there were times they did not. In an article in *Sports Illustrated*, one of Landry's coaching adversaries said, "All I can say is if Tom Landry is a Christian, then the Lord help the Lions." It was evident that to the person who uttered that statement, Tom Landry was a man who exhibited excellence, not simply in achievement but also in character.

OUR STEWARDSHIP OF TIME

In the New Testament we find two references to time using the Greek word *kairos* (Ephesians 5:16; Colossians 4:5, KJV). In both of those passages the apostle Paul exhorts us to "redeem the time." The idea seems to be that we should utilize our opportunities. Jesus did that, even in the process of handling interruptions. Those verses do not simply tell us to do more, now and faster. In each reference the context has to do with dealing with unbelievers, who live under the influence of a pagan world. The word translated "time" is the same term translated "season" in Paul's exhortation to Timothy to be "instant" in season and out of season (2 Timothy 4:2, KJV). To be "instant" means to be prepared. The idea of redeeming the time, a phrase that literally means "to buy back," is the idea of freeing our time. It is not simply packing life with more activity, even in ministry. Rather, it involves developing balance in our lives so that we can utilize opportunities that come our way.

There is so much we want to do, so much that needs to be done, and so much that society insists we must do. As one O-C housewife put it, "We must not have ring around the collar. We must have floors that gleam until we can see our faces in them. We must have furniture that reflects an arranged bouquet in living color. We must be gourmet cooks, publicly aware, socially active, and academically and intellectually current."

Our obsessive minds can easily operate on a strictly scheduled basis, but we need to allow ourselves to incorporate opportunity. In *How to Have All the Time You Need Every Day,* Pat King says of interruptions, "When we drop our list and change our plans for His work . . . He more than makes up for the time given." She goes on to observe that from her experience almost miraculously everything on her list winds up being accomplished anyway [(Wheaton, Ill.: Tyndale, 1980] p. 49).

Jesus invested significant time in solitude. On one of the busiest days in His life, He dealt with the multitudes, taught with authority, case out demons, and faced an entire village of people with incredible needs (Mark 1:32-33). The following morning the Savior made it a priority to arise before daylight and depart to a solitary place to pray. He did not neglect His mission in life (v. 38). But He did make prayer—time alone with His Father—a priority. Jesus spells out what is a genuinely important priority: "Seek first his kingdom and his righteousness, and all these things will be given to you as well" (Matthew 6:33).

THE ETERNAL PERSPECTIVE

To move beyond burnout an individual must develop the ability to live life in light of eternity rather than within the constraints of time. No one has captured that concept quite as well as Moses. Moses' life was marked by many significant events. He was born with great disadvantages but under supernatural circumstances; he was raised with a "silver spoon" in his mouth. But he chose to suffer affliction with the people of God rather than to enjoy the pleasures of sin for a short time (Hebrews 11:25).

Following an easy life in Egypt as the son of Pharaoh's daughter, Moses spent forty years caring for a small herd of sheep on the backside of the desert. Yet God called him from tending sheep to lead a flock of more than two million Israelites from Egypt to the land He had promised them.

Moses' final thoughts summarizing his life are found in Psalm 90. Here he makes two significant observations. First, *God is eternal, though man is finite.* For every generation, God has served as the *ma'on,* the "refuge" or "dwelling place." Every human being is a transient, a pilgrim; yet God predates the mountains and the inhabited world. He is the God who is "from everlasting to everlasting" (v. 2). Just as the Israelites were pilgrims, so we who live in the closing decade of the twentieth century will only be here for a short time.

Second, Moses observes that *because man is sinful, God is a God of wrath.* Utilizing vivid language to describe man's finiteness, Moses further notes that the all-knowing God is fully aware of our perverseness and even knows the secret imperfections that are part of the "tale" of our lives. It is the result of sin that we become slaves to the clock and the calendar. Whether we live seven years or seventy, ultimately we will all experience death (v. 10).

Moses articulated a principle that we need to remember when we face discouraging circumstances: "Teach us to number our days aright, that we may gain a heart of wisdom" (v. 12). When Moses wrote those words, the number of his days had grown exceedingly short. He knew his time was at hand. In the time he had left he wanted to make the most of each day of life.

As we follow the example for living Jesus provided us, we can better order our priorities and align our lives to those things that matter most. Jesus' life exhibited an eternal quality because He lived with eternal values in view. As we set our life's goals, we need to adopt His perspective and thereby find skill in handling the unpredictable circumstances of life.

14
BEYOND DEATH—
THE LAST ENEMY

After years of successfully managing the New York Yankees, Dick Howser reached the pinnacle of his managerial career in 1985 when he led the Kansas City Royals to a dramatic seventh-game World Series victory over the St. Louis Cardinals. A man of small stature yet boundless energy, Howser had seemingly reached the top.

The following year he led the American League All Stars to a 3 to 2 victory over the National League squad. Although no one knew it at the time, that was to be Dick Howser's last appearance as a major league manager. Shortly afterward he complained of serious pain and was hospitalized. Surgery revealed a malignant brain tumor. Although Howser attempted a comeback, he eventually announced his resignation just before the start of the 1987 season.

Less than eleven months after reaching the pinnacle of his career, Dick Howser died on June 17, 1987.

During the long months of struggling against his debilitating illness, he did not allow the prospect of death to defeat him. The day after Howser's death, *Kansas City Star* sports writer Gib Twyman described him as a man who focused "on the positive, the upbeat, a high note as high as heaven itself." Twyman quoted Howser as saying, "God has already told me I'm going to heaven. I know I'm going to be happy." In fact, three weeks before he died, Howser turned to his best friend, Trevor Grubbs, and said, "Jesus wants me to come home. It would be fine if He took me today."

NUMBERING OUR DAYS

What gave Dick Howser victory over death? He had learned to number his days and apply his heart to wisdom. All of us will eventually face death. If we, like Dick Howser, are to have victory over death, we also must learn to number our days and apply our hearts to wisdom. Why is it important to "number our days"? Several reasons are given in Psalm 90. Moses prays in verse 14, "Satisfy us in the morning with your unfailing love, that we may sing for joy and be glad all our days." We need to number our days, to be satisfied with God's unfailing loyal love, so that our joy in life each day will be the more complete. When we "number our days" we will also be able to balance the sorrow of affliction with gladness from God. Moses experienced many difficult times in his life, but God balanced those difficulties with blessings. As Christians we can expect lasting, genuine gladness in our relationship with Him.

Finally, numbering our days will give us a legacy that outlives this present life. Our lives, properly invested, can produce lasting fruitfulness.

During the summer of 1987 a number of men met with Dr. James Dobson and other members of Focus on the Family at El Canyon Ranch in Montana for a week-long retreat of fellowship and mutual encouragement. After the retreat, four men from Dallas, Texas, boarded a twin-engine Cessna 421 to return home. They never made it.

Three days later rescue workers found the bodies in the wrecked aircraft in a treeless area of the Shoshone National Forest fifteen miles west of Kote, Wyoming. The impact of the deaths of those men jolted the Dallas-Fort Worth area. Local media provided extensive coverage. Thousands gathered to pay tribute at a joint memorial service at which Dr. Dobson gave an eternal perspective:

> Would you not have enjoyed being there when these men made the transition to the other side? The Lord greeted them and wrapped His arms around them. Creath was laughing. I know he was. And Hugo was talking in that Texas accent that most of us couldn't understand very well. Knowing them as I did, I can hear them saying, "But Lord, what about our families?" And I know the Lord gave them the assurance that He is going to be with you all —and He will. . . . Your fathers are alive, and we will see them again some day. [*Focus on the Family,* September 1987]

They were men whose lives had made incredible impacts; yet their deaths made equally great impacts.

So it was in 1956 when Jim Elliot and four other men were martyred by Auca Indians in South America. Willing to invest their lives in service far from home, they were ultimately called, as the apostle Paul expressed it, to pour out their lives as sacrifice (Philippians 2:17). Some time before his death Jim Elliot had written his wife-to-be, Elisabeth, of his philosophy of life: "Wherever you are, be all there. Live to the hilt each day what you believe to be the will of God." That is how Jim Elliot and his colleagues lived, and that is how they died. Through the impact of their deaths, literally hundreds of young men and women responded to the call to serve Jesus Christ in foreign missions.

Like Jim Elliot and the other martyred men, we must live with eternity in view. Why? Because we never know when we will pass from this life into eternity.

ACCOMPLISHING GOD'S PURPOSES

Moses taught also that it is important to build meaning and beauty into the daily routine of life and to temper it with a lasting work consistent with the purpose of God. Moses left a legacy. The same perspective motivated a brilliant Benjaminite named Saul of Tarsus who became the apostle Paul of the New Testament, a man whose life ministry was wrapped up in the goal of serving Jesus Christ and telling others about Him.

In 2 Corinthians Paul captures the essence of his perspective on ministry. His observations were set in the context of his statement in 1 Corinthians 4:11 that we are "homeless," or as the King James Version puts it, we "have no certain dwelling-place." Paul, like Moses, considered himself a pilgrim, and he devoted his life to serving the Savior who had called him.

Second Corinthians 4:7-12 provides Paul's explanation for and defense of his ministry. It is an insightful passage that captures lessons about God's purposes in our lives. After describing the glory of the ministry to which he was called, Paul gave a threefold perspective as to why his life was meaningful.

PAUL DEPENDED ON GOD'S STRENGTH

Looking at his circumstances, Paul noted that ministry or service for God, though glorious, is accomplished in human bodies, which are essentially "jars of clay." Thus, instead of rejoicing in our abilities, we need to recognize "the excellence of the power [to] be of God and not of us" (v. 7, NKJV*).

* *New King James Version.*

Later, in the same book, Paul refers to a thorn in his flesh, a physical adversity about which he prayed three times for relief. He finally came to recognize the problem as God's way of telling him, "My grace is sufficient for you, for My strength is made perfect in weakness" (2 Corinthians 12:9, NKJV).

Furthermore, although Paul was surrounded by adversity he looked beyond the circumstances of this life. He had been troubled on every side—perplexed, persecuted, and cast down—yet he never entertained the idea of giving up. He felt pressured but not abandoned. He was down but never rendered inoperative. We find the reason in 2 Corinthians 4:10-11: Paul considered himself to have been given all of God's life, power, and resources to cope with his present distress. Ultimately, God's purpose was to use both good and bad circumstances to demonstrate the life of Jesus in Paul's mortal flesh (v. 11).

PAUL FOCUSED ON GOD'S PROVISION

Paul focused on God's provision. In 2 Corinthians 4:12-13 he speaks of faith, using a quote from Psalm 116:10. We have the same spirit of faith manifested by the psalmist who said, "I believed; therefore I said." We are to trust God today, one day at a time.

Paul directs us also to focus on hope. That is implied in verses 14-15. That hope is based specifically on the resurrection of the Savior. Paul points out in 1 Corinthians 15:23 that Jesus is the "firstfruits," which gives us not only the hope of resurrection beyond death, but also the anticipation of being presented together with other believers in the presence of God. Thus, not only can I trust God for today; I can trust Him for tomorrow as well.

PAUL HAD PERSPECTIVE ON GOD'S PURPOSE

Moving beyond faith and hope, Paul concludes his perspective on God's purpose in verses 16-18. Here we find three timely exhortations to help the obsessive-compulsive person live in light of eternity.

1. *Fight to the finish.* We must never give up. Paul says, "We do not lose heart. Though outwardly we are wasting away, yet inwardly we are being renewed day by day" (2 Corinthians 4:16). Note the emphasis on living life one day at a time. Every day brings with it another opportunity not to give up and to live life joyfully one day at a time. In the book of Acts we see Paul's resolve not to allow circumstances to shake him: "None of these things move me" (Acts 20:24a, KJV).

Such perspective is consistent with Jesus' purpose for His disciples: "that they should always pray and not give up" (Luke 18:1). During the darkest days of World War II, Sir Winston Churchill gave his countrymen a brief but poignant message: "We must never, never, never, never quit."

2. *Weigh your life.* We must evaluate the present in light of eternity. We often hear the phrases "weigh the difference" or "weigh the options." Paul encourages us to weigh the afflictions of life against the glory of eternity. Paul measured the intensity of suffering against the ultimate glory and the length of present suffering against the duration of eternity.

As a result he was able to look at his personal sufferings as "light" and "momentary" (cf. 2 Corinthians 11). For Paul, comparing the present with eternity was like comparing a pocketful of copper pennies with a large trunk of thousand-dollar bills. Centuries before Paul, the Hebrew prophet Jeremiah wrote about the reality of daily living, sharing words that sustained him through the darkest hours of Israel's history: "Yet this I call to mind and therefore I have hope: Because of the Lord's great love we are not consumed, for his compassions never fail. They are new every morning; great is your faithfulness" (Lamentations 3:21-23).

3. *Keep an eye on eternity.* We must look beyond the temporal to the eternal. The word Paul uses for "look" (2 Corinthians 4:18) is not the word generally used. Instead he uses the Greek word *scopos,* from which we derive the English word "scope," as in a telescope or the scope of a rifle. Paul uses this term to describe a sharply focused look that does not consider anything outside that focus. Picture a man on a bluff in Colorado focusing his rifle on a large bull elk several hundred yards down a slope. Other things are happening around the man—birds are chattering, wildlife is moving, sunlight is filtering through the trees. But the hunter is not deterred by those potential distractions. His eye, his trigger finger, his shoulder, and his very being concentrate only on the hunted game he observes through his scope.

In the same way Paul tells us we are to focus beyond our temporal circumstances onto that which is eternal. That is precisely what the author of Hebrews had in mind when he said, "Let us run with perseverance the race marked out for us. Let us fix our eyes on Jesus, the author and perfecter of our faith" (12:1b-2). Peter provided us with a vivid illustration of this truth when he requested of the Lord that he might walk on water (Matthew 14:28-29). Most of us long ago learned that walking on water isn't something the average person can do, even on a perfectly calm body of water. Yet, in the midst of a violent storm Peter said, "Lord, if it's you . . . tell me to come to you on the water" (v. 28). As long as Peter kept his eyes on the Lord, he was able to step across the waves as though they were pavement. But when he took his eyes off the Savior and noticed, as the King James Version puts it, that "the wind was boisterous," Peter began to sink.

The obvious lesson for us is that maintaining perspective involves keeping our eyes on the Savior. That is how Moses kept going: "He persevered because he saw him who is invisible" (Hebrews 11:27). That is how Paul endured the adversities he faced in life. And that is the perspective that can pull us through life's trials.

One test of how we handle adversity is what we do when we lose possessions. With many of us obsessive-compulsives, maintaining hold of possessions is an important factor in life. That is because we often have the wrong perspective on success. We frequently view success as determined by what car we drive or how we look. Many of us have a dress-for-success mentality. Webster defines success as "the attainment of wealth, favor, or eminence." Michael Corta, in his book *Power! How to Get It, How to Use It,* says, "All life is a game of power. The object of the game is simple enough—to know what you want and get it."

Our society places a strong emphasis on "getting." We become consumers geared toward the lust of the flesh, often overeating and harming the temple of the Holy Spirit. We also have become caught up in the lust of the eyes, going on shopping sprees, waving our plastic credit cards, grabbing far more than we ever need. We become caught up in the pride of life, proud of our designer clothes, our carefully manicured hands, and our landscaped lawns. Yet, according to 1 John 2, all those things are temporal.

Certainly it is appropriate for us to enjoy our possessions. First Timothy 6:17 tells us that we can enjoy the world without loving it. We are to be content to have our basic life needs met (v. 8), but at the same time we must avoid the temptation and harmful consequences of the overwhelming desire to be rich (v. 9). We are to flee from coveting material possessions but should pursue virtuous character (v. 11). Though the world has a "go for it" mentality regarding possessions, our focus should be on "the eternal life to which [we] were called" (v. 12).

An obsession for acquiring money can be a major problem for many obsessive-compulsives, who have a strong need for security and tend to be materialistic. Sadly, rather than bringing security, the love of money is likely instead to lead to burnout. The Bible teaches that we are not to trust in material possessions. Rather, we are to trust in the living God and be thankful for His provisions as we strive to live godly lives in light of eternity. God requires that we be good stewards of our resources. Moving beyond burnout involves having the right perspective on financial matters.

Stanley Marcus of Neiman-Marcus, in a *Dallas Morning News* column titled "Burnout: A Passing of the Buck," wrote, "Today psychological wiring on fire is everywhere." Marcus relates burnout to a "declaration of bankruptcy—something necessary but often irresponsible and undignified." He stated that the word *burnout* gained increased use in Texas during the current oil-induced recession of the late 1980s. According to Marcus, blaming burnout allows us to pass the buck to other people and circumstances rather than forcing us to learn to overcome life's obstacles. In short, Marcus says, we need to exercise responsibility before burnout occurs.

THE BOTTOM LINE

The bottom line in facing adversity is to understand that God has a gracious purpose for allowing us to experience suffering. Job saw that purpose and drew three important observations from his experience (Job 23:10).

1. *God knows what is happening to me.* I am not isolated from God. "He knows the way that I take" (v. 10). For many years the football field at the University of Alabama was dominated by a twenty-foot tower. Brian Newman, a therapist at our clinic and an Alabama alumnus, remembers that tower as the place where legendary coach Paul "Bear" Bryant spent the hours of football practice. While Bryant's assistants worked with the offense, defense, and special teams, Coach Bryant carefully observed from his tower. He always knew what was happening; he knew when the players were doing well and when they were not.

In similar fashion, God in heaven sees and knows every facet of our every experience. We can take comfort in the fact that nothing escapes His omniscient scrutiny.

2. *God uses circumstances to discipline us.* He is not an angry, punitive Father in heaven trying to bring us harm. But He may put us to the test. Job said of God, "He has tested me" (v. 10b). One of the authors played football in high school. His first two weeks of summer practice under the hot sun were an unforgiving introduction to the world of athletic conditioning. One session of leg lifts seemed especially brutal. The coach quietly encouraged the players, "Think of the good things in life." To which one of the players replied, "There aren't any." The coach said, "Sure there are. In a couple of weeks you'll be able to do this with no pain." Sure enough, two weeks later the coach's prediction proved to be correct.

3. *God uses a process to refine us and reflect His glory.* That is the ultimate purpose for this life. Job was reminded that he would "come forth as gold" (v. 10c). Some suffering is unnecessary. We do not need to fall into the trap of becoming victims. And there is suffering we bring upon ourselves as the consequences of our sins (1 Peter 4).

At other times adversity simply happens. And when it does, we need to have the appropriate attitude. Thankfulness should be a significant portion of that attitude. In Psalm 103 the psalmist reminds us to remember all of God's benefits. Throughout the book of Deuteronomy we find the words "remember" and "forget."

Thankfulness is therapeutic. Many times the authors of this book have recommended that individuals who feel overwhelmed by their problems make a list of the positive things for which they are thankful. We have also recommended that they maintain a "blessing" journal as a long-term project and that they regularly review the benefits catalogued in that journal.

We need to encourage and motivate thankfulness in others. Three references in the book of Proverbs indicate that others benefit when we adopt a positive, optimistic outlook on life (15:13, 15; 17:22). Our disposition affects both our own well-being and the well-being of those around us.

Another significant element of attitude is a positive spirit. Note that in Proverbs a "merry heart" is not the mirth of modern comedians or fools. The idea of *merry* means "joyful" or "good" in the sense of "pleasant" or "happy." The heart is one of the most important concepts in the Old Testament. This component of our personality can have a strong influence, for the condition of the heart leaves its stamp on the appearance and the activity of an individual.

A merry heart produces a pleasant countenance (Proverbs 15:13). This pleasant countenance in turn produces a festive outlook on life (v. 15). It is interesting to note that the contrast in this verse is not between the poor and the rich, but rather between the poor and the poor. A person may spend each evening eating at upscale restaurants, yet feel miserable. Another person, however, may be able to look at a trip to McDonald's as the ultimate eating experience.

In addition, a merry heart can actually produce good health (17:22). Psychiatric research has noted that more than 50 percent of all hospital beds have a significant emotional component in the diagnosis of the patients who occupy them. Why? Because the emotional affects the physical, and the spiritual can affect both. Yet so often we allow the circumstances of life to crush our spirits. It is interesting that in James 5 the concepts of a merry heart and good health both appear within the context of sickness. "Is anyone happy? Let him sing songs of praise. Is any one of you sick? He should call the elders of the church to pray over him and anoint him with oil in the name of the Lord" (vv. 13b-14). Developing a merry heart and encouraging it in others can lead to good health.

It is also important, especially for Type A's and perfectionists, to balance the long and short views of circumstances. One of the contrasts we have examined is between the quantity-oriented Type A and the quality-oriented perfectionist. The Type A often tends to jump into too many tasks and develop that as a style of relating. Often he does not think of the long-term consequences of that decision.

Mike, a typical obsessive-compulsive businessman, was offered a new position with his company, plus a substantial increase in pay. Without consulting anyone for advice or input—or even discussing the matter with his wife or family—Mike made his decision. Soon the moving van arrived and Mike's family and belongings were transported to a new home thousands of miles away.

Sadly, however, Mike hadn't considered the long-term consequences of his decision. His wife became depressed because she lacked friends. The children began acting out in school because of the trauma of being uprooted. Mike soon ran into conflicts in his new job responsibilities. The result was devastating. Mike needed to develop a long view to better visualize the long-term consequences of his decision, either through counseling or simply by working on it himself.

On the other hand, the perfectionistic obsessive-compulsive needs to develop the short view. These people will often refuse to make a short-term decision or to take action immediately because they are so fearful of being overwhelmed by the long-term consequences of present actions.

Janice had just graduated from college with a degree in teaching, and she had the opportunity to become a skilled teacher. She was given three or four opportunities, but she wound up letting deadlines pass on all of them, instead taking a job in a grocery store. Janice was afraid that whatever decision she made would unalterably commit her to that particular job, with its strengths and weaknesses.

The O-C somehow needs to achieve balance, and, as in these examples, balance can be observed in attitude. Type A tends to have a "go for it" mentality and sometimes tends to give up and become discouraged. The perfectionist will tend to fear "going for it" but will "keep on keeping on." There is a time to go for it, and there is a time to keep on keeping on. Both the fearful perfectionist and the gung-ho Type A compulsives need to recognize that they can learn from each other.

OVERCOMING THE LAST ENEMY

In our fast-paced society, an increasing number of people are being devastated by burnout. For some people, as Stanley Marcus pointed out, blaming burnout is a cop-out. Yet simply avoiding burnout is not enough. Life should not consist of mere existence or mediocrity. The scriptural standard is that we should be abounding. In 1 Corinthians 15:58 we read, "Therefore, my beloved brethren, be steadfast, immovable, always abounding in the work of the Lord, knowing that your labor is not in vain in the Lord" (NKJV). That exhortation from the apostle Paul is sometimes viewed as being for someone who works so hard that he just burns out. But that is not what the verse is saying. Nor is it describing "the abundant life" as some kind of nebulous state of being for people whose heads are in the clouds spiritually. Rather, Paul was writing to a group of very down-to-earth people who struggled with conflicts, personal holiness, proper exercise of spiritual gifts, and doctrinal truths. In other words, he was writing to real people.

The church at Corinth was a problem church. Yet Paul concluded his letter to the Corinthians with a chapter detailing the difference the resurrection of Jesus Christ made—the impact of the transforming power of the gospel. He described how the gospel and the resurrection pointed ahead to the ultimate return of Jesus Christ and how the Savior would destroy death, the last enemy. Then he gave that ultimate perspective by which to live in the meantime.

How are we to live? Paul told the Corinthians, whom he loved, three things he wanted them to be: steadfast, immovable, and abounding.

BE STEADFAST

The primary connotation of the word *steadfast* (Greek, *hedraios*) is regarding something seated or set in place. It is used in Colossians 1:2 of one who is doctrinally settled, grounded in the faith with a firm foundation. The steadfast individual has doctrinal, moral, and spiritual moorings and is solidly connected to God and His Word.

The ups and downs of the world often strike like waves rocking a boat. If the boat is firmly secured, even a storm cannot destroy it. Some time ago a storm struck a sheltered Caribbean bay in which a number of fishing boats had sought shelter. The clouds lowered, the winds kicked up, and the force of the waves was quite ferocious. However, the fishing boats were solidly tied with heavy rope to the dock; pilings had been driven deep into the ground, and the boats were firmly connected so that no action of the wind or waves could break the boats from their moorings.

BE IMMOVABLE

The next word takes our perspective a step further. "Immovable" (Greek, *ametakinetos*) carries the idea of "being firm" and is used only here in the New Testament. However, in Colossians 1:23, the positive form of the word is used along with the same term for "steadfast" to mean not moved away from the hope of the gospel. A related word is translated "the water is stirred" (John 5:7). This word has the idea of something being displaced or moved from one place to another. It was used in the Old Testament to prohibit transferring a landmark from one place to another (Deuteronomy 19:14, Septuagint). It was also used to mean "put . . . to flight" (Deuteronomy 32:30; Isaiah 22:3, Septuagint). When boats are not anchored and steadfast they can be moved from one place to another. So it is with people.

BE ABOUNDING

The prerequisite to abounding is to be steadfast and unmovable. However, it is not enough just to be firmly fixed in one place. God's goal for believers is that we may be always abounding. The implication of the term "always" seems to be "on every occasion." Paul brought this out several times in his writings to the Thessalonians:

"Be joyful *always*" (1 Thessalonians 5:16, emphasis added).

Paul gave thanks for them *always* (1 Thessalonians 1:2; 2 Thessalonians 1:3; emphasis added).

He *always* prayed for them (2 Thessalonians 1:11, emphasis added).

The significant term for moving beyond burnout is "abounding" (Greek, *perisseuo*). It was a common term in the vernacular of Paul's day. It meant something that was present in overabundance. Paul was fond of this term. At times he intensified it to "superabounding" as in Romans 5:20, 2 Corinthians 7:4, and Ephesians 3:20. In fact, an examination of Paul's writings reveals areas in which we are to be abounding.

- We are to abound in hope (Romans 15:13).
- We are to abound in unconditional love for others (1 Thessalonians 4:10). Yet this love is to abound within the parameters of knowledge and discernment (Philippians 1:9).

- We are to abound in thanksgiving (Colossians 2:7).
- We are to abound in the grace of giving, or generosity (2 Corinthians 8:7).

The Corinthians abounded in faith, in utterance, in knowledge, in diligence, and in love. Likewise, our lives are to be characterized by abundant growth and an abounding walk that continues to please God in increasing measure (1 Thessalonians 4:1).

In addition, we are to abound in the work of the Lord. Being thankful for what God has given us helps us to do that. First Thessalonians 5:18 talks about always giving thanks. Psalm 103:2 reads, "Praise the Lord, O my soul, and forget not all his benefits." Not only do we need to express thankfulness to God, but we must *maintain* this attitude as well. Our lists should include thanks for hope, the work of the Lord, unconditional love, generosity, and our walk.

For the individual who experiences burnout, all of life is fruitless and pointless. Labor is hard and frustrating. Solomon, the author of Ecclesiastes, poured himself into many areas of endeavor, but found each to be futile. "Yet when I surveyed all that my hands had done and what I had toiled to achieve, everything was meaningless, a chasing after the wind; nothing was gained under the sun" (Ecclesiastes 2:11). Yet the individual who has moved beyond burnout will acknowledge that a great deal of life involves work.

In fact, life actually is a sort of hard labor, the kind of toil that results in weariness. Yet it is labor with a purpose, not labor in vain. The phrase "in vain" is like an empty jar. Picture an individual who has worked very hard in a garden under the baking sun and is desperately thirsty. He returns to his house, opens the refrigerator door, and sees what appears to be a jar filled with water. He reaches for the jar and finds it is empty.

In Christ, life is neither empty nor in vain; it is meaningful and refreshing—even when circumstances seem exceedingly hard. Paul emphatically declares that the individual who is steadfast, immovable, and abounding will be firmly fixed, rooted, and planted in life.

FINISHING THE RACE

In light of the victory we have over death through Jesus Christ, we need to remain firmly fixed in our faith. Growing toward maturity requires that we do not quit. Rather, we need consistently to pursue excellence in our service for Jesus Christ and our relationship with Him, knowing that there is both present and eternal benefit, even though at times life may be hard. To avoid burnout it is imperative that we live one day at a time. That means we cannot approach life as a fifty-yard dash. Instead, we must view life as a ten-kilometer race, which we have our entire lives to run.

None of us knows how many days we will be given in this life. We are to live as though death could come any day while we focus on the long haul. That way we will grow old God's way—better, not bitter. Paul said we are to live life so as to "finish [our] course with joy" (Acts 20:24, KJV). When we have achieved our goal—moving beyond burnout toward healthy, abundant living—we will be able to say with the apostle Paul, "I have fought the good fight, I have finished the race" (2 Timothy 4:7). We can do that by being committed to a wholehearted love for God, an unconditional love for people, and a loose grip on our possessions.

As we seek to align our daily priorities and our life goals with God's eternal values, we will become more conditioned and better prepared for eternity. Death will lose its sting. Like Dick Howser, we can look ahead with anticipation to the day Jesus takes us home, yet continue to live life abundantly, one day at a time, with joy.

GLOSSARY

ACTING-OUT

This term describes how some individuals use action as a response to unconscious conflicts. Often instead of responding to insight, a person relieves the repressed emotions by undertaking some kind of behavior, which is usually aggressive, antisocial, or otherwise inappropriate. For example, a young lady who has repressed anger toward her father may act out that anger by becoming sexually promiscuous; or a man with unconscious hostility toward his father may become physically aggressive toward his boss.

BURNOUT

A cluster of symptoms, including emotional exhaustion, depersonalization, or a desire to withdraw from people, and reduced accomplishment (working harder and harder while accomplishing less and less). Although current stresses contribute to burnout, other significant factors include obsessive-compulsive or perfectionistic personality traits and bitterness or unresolved anger.

COMPULSION

A seemingly irresistible urge to carry out an action or ritual series of actions. Closely related to obsession, the anxiety that leads to the compulsion stems from ideas or obsessions that may be unacceptable to the individual but nonetheless force their way into conscious awareness. The compulsion displaces attention from the obsessions, thus relieving anxiety. Common compulsions include checking and rechecking locks, or repeated handwashing.

CONFLICT

The presence of divergent goals or aims within an individual, between two individuals, or within a group. Internal conflict may involve such competing feelings as the need for autonomy versus the need to be dependent on a partner, or a highly positive, idealistic view of self conflicting with a despising attitude toward self. One kind of conflict is termed approach-approach, when a person is attracted toward two desirable but mutually-exclusive goals. Also common is approach-avoidance conflict, where a strong attraction (purchasing a beautiful new home) may be balanced by a strong aversion (increased indebtedness). Conflict between individuals is frequently intensified when one individual wishes to cooperate while the other views the situation as competitive. The ability to function is usually improved as conflict is reduced.

CYCLOTHYMIC

The cyclothymic personality tends to experience intense ups and downs. Such individuals may feel highly elated for a period of time, then experience a period of deep depression. When high, a cyclothymic person is generally cheerful, humorous, and outgoing, though sometimes anger or sarcasm surface. In the depressed stage the same individual may appear sad, hopeless, helpless, despondent, or unable to perform.

Periods of highs and lows may fluctuate rapidly, or they may persist over an extended period of time. Some individuals may spend the majority of their time in a depressed state, whereas others may tend to remain in the energetic high. Some individuals exhibit high energy and high achievement most of their lives and may be referred to as having "hypomanic" personalities.

HYPER-CALVINISTIC

This term is frequently used in theological circles to describe individuals who take the teachings of John Calvin to an extreme, particularly their emphasis on the sovereign control of God over the universe. Such individuals see little use in exercising the human will, praying, or encouraging others to make decisions since, "after all, God controls everything." Usually strong psychological dependency underlies this theological perspective.

HYSTERIC OR HISTRIONIC

A cluster of personality traits including a tendency toward immaturity, feelings that are intensely expressed but shallow, difficulty with interpersonal relationships, and an inclination toward the overdramatic. The Diagnostic Manual DSM III-R uses the term *histrionic*, which is derived from the Latin term for actor, *histrio*. Individuals with such personality traits may be charming and socially active, yet they also have difficulty with deep or intimate relationships. They may be demanding and manipulative. Frequently internal sexual conflict, such as unresolved anger with the parent of the opposite sex, may be present. The terms *hysteric* and *histrionic* are often used interchangeably.

OBSESSION

A persistently recurring thought or feeling, usually involuntary and inconsistent with the individual's conscious character. Obsessions usually originate in conscious attempts to deny certain unconscious desires or anxieties. Often an obsession will lead to a consuming preoccupation with philosophical or theological questions such as whether the individual has committed the unpardonable sin. Obsessions generally lead to compulsions.

OBSESSIVE-COMPULSIVE

Individuals with this particular cluster of personality traits tend to be conscientious, self-sacrificing, organized, perfectionistic, and devout. Such individuals are driven by repetitive persistent ideas or obsessions that intrude into conscious thought. Frequently their content is the opposite of what the individual would think voluntarily. Such obsessions lead to compulsions, or repetitive behaviors that are often performed ritualistically.

Obsessive-compulsive personality types commonly experience a wide range of difficulties, including perfectionism, Type A behavior, burnout, clinical depression, anxiety attacks or phobias, and even suicidal thinking. Drinking, gambling, sexual disorders or overeating are often classed as obsessive-compulsive behaviors. Obsessive-compulsive tendencies can be present in degrees ranging from mild to such severity that the life of the individual is disrupted. Gaining and acting on insight into the origin of the obsessions and compulsions can help the obsessive-compulsive personality strengthen his strengths while working on his weaknesses.

Those with intense obsessive-compulsive traits may gain help through appropriate psychiatric medications, since obsessions and compulsions are currently seen as an expression of the brain's tendency to form repetitive or circular response patterns when certain alarm responses are inadequately dampened. Medication can frequently eliminate these "short circuits," bringing important relief.

PARANOID

Individuals with paranoid personality traits tend to be suspicious, argumentative, hypersensitive, and jealous. Frequently they blame others for shortcomings and conflicts. Often the paranoid person is unreasonably jealous and may have delusions of persecution or of grandeur. Some individuals with a paranoid disorder may have an intense, unshakable system of grandiose or persecutory delusions in one area, yet may be remarkably logical and functional in other areas. Usually the paranoid individual feels an intense lack of self-worth, which has grown out of long-term stress, abuse, or rejection. An important aspect of the paranoid personality is inability or difficulty with personal trust.

PASSIVE-AGGRESSIVE PERSONALITY

Individuals with this cluster of personality traits handle underlying emotions such as anger with passive action, which tends to disrupt both work and relationships. A typical passive-aggressive individual tends to procrastinate, obstruct, forget, and dawdle, while denying that such behavior is in any way intentionally oppositional. Often this individual may be negative, sullen, pessimistic, disinterested, or stubborn. While obstructing those around them, such individuals often seem unaware of the effects of their behavior. Passive-aggressive personality traits are often a hostile response to prolonged or intense dependency. In some cases the strong dependency needs of the passive-aggressive personality may leave such individuals susceptible to substance abuse.

PERFECTIONIST

This individual frequently has a large number of obsessive-compulsive personality traits that remind him: (1) of the concept of the ideal or perfect and (2) that he, himself, utterly fails to measure up to perfection. Often we see in perfectionists a combination of obsessive-compulsive and passive-aggressive personality traits, as seen in the example of the college student who discards a carefully researched and laboriously typed paper because of one small typographical error near the end of the document. Christian perfectionists frequently misunderstand or misinterpret the concept of perfection. In our Bibles such Greek words as *teleos* or *artios* are translated "perfect," but they actually refer to maturity or growth. For the believer, perfectionism can be dealt with by delving into its hidden roots, by restructuring of ideals so that they correspond more closely with reality, by persistence in spiritual and emotional growth, and by placing our expectations on Christ rather than on ourselves or others. Although those who are Christians will ultimately become perfect in Christ, perfection will never occur in present human experience.

PERSONALITY TRAITS

The term "personality" is one of the more abstract concepts in the English language. It originates from the classical Latin term *persona*, which described the mask an actor wore in a play. *Personality traits refer to specific characteristics in an individual which, when taken together, give substance to the personality and allow one to categorize generally the individual with others who have similar characteristics.* Personality traits are the concrete differences that make individuals unique but that also mark individuals as similar.

Personality reflects the image of God, whereas individual traits may represent strengths to be strengthened or weaknesses to be worked on.

SCHIZOPHRENIA

A clinical disorder marked by a thorough disturbance of feeling, mood, and thought involving psychotic breaks with reality. Classical symptoms have been described as involving "4 A's": flat or inappropriate facial affect, loose associations, autism, and ambivalent features. Other symptoms may include delusions—beliefs held to be true in the face of solid evidence to the contrary—and hallucinations—hearing, seeing, or feeling things that are not present.

Schizophrenia generally occurs in about 8 to 10 of every 1,000 people. Treatment involves medication, psychotherapy, community support, and stress management, which tends to exacerbate schizophrenic breaks.

SELF-TALK

The internal process by which we give ourselves feedback and messages on an ongoing basis. Self-talk can be either negative or positive, accurate or inaccurate. Many individuals become conditioned to give themselves inaccurate, negative, and debilitating messages that are destructive in nature. Such negative self-talk often incorporates such distorted thinking as:

Magnification: "This is a terrible, horrible
disaster!"

Selective attention: "This single low test grade out-
weighs all my other positive scores put together."

Personalization: "He's rejecting me. I must be a terrible failure."

Polarized thinking: "I have to be either totally good,
or I'm totally bad."

Overgeneralization: "I can never do anything
right. Locking my keys in the car today just
proves it."

Insight into the underlying reasons for our negative self-talk (such as parental conditioning) coupled
with cognitive restructuring can help turn self-talk
into a positive tool rather than a negative habit.

SEPTUAGINT

*A Greek translation of the Hebrew Old Testa-
ment.* It represented the first attempt to translate the
Hebrew Scriptures of the Old Testament into another
language and was accomplished in the Egyptian city of
Alexandria by seventy or seventy-two elders, according
to tradition. LXX (meaning the Septuagint) is an ab-
breviation representing the numeral 70.) Ultimately
the Christian church in Alexandria began using the Al-
exandrian Septuagint, and Christian scholars still utilize it as an important resource for studying the Old
Testament today.

TYPE A

*Commonly associated with the obsessive-com-
pulsive personality, Type A generally refers to a cluster of traits representing a person of high energy and
intense activity.* Type A personalities are prone to car-

diac and other health risks; sometimes they are described as having "hurry sickness."

Coupled with the tendency to rush through almost everything in life, Type A's frequently exhibit symptoms of underlying anger. The combination of those stress-inducing tendencies make Type A's a high risk for burnout.

Moody Press, a ministry of the Moody Bible Institute, is designed for education, evangelization, and edification. If we may assist you in knowing more about Christ and the Christian life, please write us without obligation: Moody Press, c/o MLM, Chicago, Illinois 60610.